SOUP SWAP

SOUP SWAP

COMFORTING RECIPES
to MAKE and SHARE

Kathy Gunst

PHOTOGRAPHS BY
Yvonne Duivenvoorden

CHRONICLE BOOKS
SAN FRANCISCO

Library of Congress Cataloging-in-Publication Data available.
ISBN 978-1-4521-4836-6

Manufactured in China

Designed by Alice Chau
Typesetting by DC Type

Food styling by Lucie Richard
Prop styling by Catherine Doherty

Chronicle books and gifts are available at special quantity discounts to corporations, professional associations, literacy programs, and other organizations. For details and discount information, please contact our premiums department at corporatesales@ chroniclebooks.com or at 1-800-759-0190.

10 9 8 7 6 5 4 3 2 1

Chronicle Books LLC
680 Second Street
San Francisco, California 94107
www.chroniclebooks.com

To John, Maya, and Emma

CONTENTS

INTRODUCTION

During one of the fiercest New England winters in recent memory, I awoke to find my kitchen door frozen shut and two of my kitchen windows totally obscured by mountains of snow. It was a long season of coping with whiteout blizzard conditions; bitter, howling winds; and record snowfalls. On one frigid but unusually sunny and clear day that winter, I was in Boston to pick up my husband at South Station when a cop banged on the roof of my car. Dutifully I rolled down the window. "Ma'am, you can't stop here," he barked. "We're in the middle of an emergency." "Emergency, officer?" I asked, imagining every terrible scenario that has ever leaped from my TV screen. "Yes, ma'am. A snow emergency! Keep moving."

Keep moving. Words that were easier said than done that winter. New Englanders are hardy when it comes to snow and cold weather, but in my three-plus decades of living here, it was a winter no one will soon forget. In late November the severe weather arrived, and it stayed clear into mid-April. But as it turned out, that winter *was* good for several things—sleeping, cross-country skiing, and making soup.

I spent several long, dark months in my kitchen creating soup recipes. I woke up thinking about soup and got back into bed at the end of a long soup-filled day reviewing the day's recipes, "Wow, that fish chowder was good. Not sure if the carrot-ginger soup has too much ginger. What if I topped the tomato soup with tiny grilled-cheese-sandwich croutons?"

One morning at six-thirty, as the sky was turning a fluorescent pink, my husband came downstairs, bleary-eyed, to find me sautéing leeks and chopping onions. "Kind of early for leeks, don't you think?" he asked, looking at me like I might have finally lost it.

We ate soup for breakfast, lunch, and dinner. I had small bowls for an afternoon pick-me-up. And let me tell you, I felt great. Soup, it turns out, is *very* healthful food.

I grew up in the '60s eating canned Campbell's Tomato Soup with grilled American cheese sandwiches. I adored canned soups for their consistent salty taste and smooth, almost mushy texture. I don't remember my mother ever making soup from scratch. In fact, I'm not sure I even understood it was something you could make until my first trip to Europe.

But I'm getting ahead of myself.

This story starts with my friend and neighbor, Hope Murphy. Five years ago, as winter was fast approaching, she called me. "I have the *best* idea," she began. As someone who is perpetually optimistic, Hope is aptly named. "I love making soup all winter," she explained, "but I get really sick of having the same leftover soup day after day. What if we had a soup-swap party?"

A what?

Of course, she had thought it all through. "We invite six food-loving couples and meet once a month during the winter. One couple hosts, and each of the other couples brings a homemade soup. The hosts provide a side dish, such as a salad, along with a loaf of crusty bread and a dessert—and we have a party. Then we all go home with different soups to enjoy all week. No one gets bored with just one pot of leftovers."

The deal was that everyone had to love to cook and that we would only invite friends who weren't on special diets. (We love vegans, vegetarians, and our dairy- and gluten-free friends, but sometimes you just don't want to alter a menu.) Half a decade later, the Second Sunday Soup Swap Suppers (Hope doesn't pass up a chance for alliteration) are alive and well. They have become a ritual we all look forward to.

The first soups that appeared at our swaps were excellent, but they were what you might expect—tomato, chicken noodle, and a lot of purées. As we got into soup-making season, however, the sophistication and depth of taste (and skill) evolved. Suddenly, we were sharing bowls of Thai Red Curry–Chicken Noodle Soup (page 94), Scottish-Style Smoked Haddock and Leek Chowder (page 149), Vietnamese-Style Asparagus Soup with Noodles and Spicy Peanut Paste (page 46), and Provençal-Style Fish Soup with Rouille

(page 138). Was it peer pressure? Having a long winter to focus on something? Or maybe we were all becoming master soup-makers?

Soup swaps can happen anywhere, with any number of people. I wrote an article for *Yankee* magazine a few years back about our suppers and have since met people who have told me that after reading the piece, they started their own soup swaps. They formed their own groups—with coworkers, fitness buddies, book-group members, fellow teachers, single pals, and others—and simply used the venues at hand—the office, yoga class, meeting room, school teacher's lounge, and so on.

These dinners yielded several unexpected gifts. Winter seemed shorter and more exciting. Taking on the challenge of becoming a "soup master" gave a new dimension to a season that can seem like it lasts forever here in New England. And for some people, making soup led them to a more healthful diet. The parents of two young kids told me how they used to rely on canned soup (full of sodium and preservatives) for snacks and family dinners, and how the soup suppers changed their kids' attitudes toward soup to the point where they are now cooking and enjoying homemade soups as a family.

But perhaps the biggest surprise of all was the sense of community that these soup dinners built. *Community* can mean a lot of things; your neighbors, your friends, your colleagues, members of your temple or church. When we started the soup-swap suppers, the twelve of us had just a few things in common: We all loved to cook.

And we all knew Hope and her husband, Brad. Although we all lived within thirty minutes of one another and some of us were already friendly, there were others we knew only slightly. Turns out, there is a camaraderie that comes from sharing soup on cold winter evenings that has tied us together in an unlikely bond. Our circle of soup-loving friends has grown to be much more than a once-a-month gathering at a dinner party.

Over the years, we have developed rituals. At one supper, we decided that our soups needed to be introduced before we dove into our bowls. Each cook briefly described the ingredients that went into the soup and the source of his or her inspiration. The tone of these introductions always reminds me of a therapy group, "Hello, my name is Kathy, and tonight I made a roasted winter vegetable soup with a parsley pesto because when I was a kid we always . . ." Some might consider this ritual pretentious, but it became great fun.

Our budding "soup masters" started shopping at farmers' markets (yes, northern New England is full of winter farmers' markets) in order to make soup with locally sourced ingredients. When we traveled for work or pleasure, we brought back soup recipes instead of souvenirs. Soup brought us together.

One of the members of our group is a cartoonist. As another ritual—and an unintentional homage to *The New Yorker*—each time we get together he brings an uncaptioned piece of work and, between spoonfuls of hot soup, we try to think of clever captions for it. At the end of the night he reads them aloud, and we howl with laughter.

I'm sure we would have developed different but equally memorable rituals if we had a poet, actor, or a musician in our group.

The first step in organizing a Soup Swap is getting over the misconception that making soup is difficult. Honestly, there are few foods that are simpler to prepare. In many cases, it's a matter of sautéing a few vegetables and herbs and adding some stock. There's a wide range of recipes in this book—from soups that can be put together in well under an hour to soups that take a good part of the day or weekend—but mostly soup does its own thing. It's like the child who is perfectly content reading a book and coloring all day, not needing much parenting from you. Set it up, show it some care, and go do something else while the soup simmers.

The great thing about this style of entertaining is that all you have to do is make one pot of soup. We alternate homes and hosting duties for every party, so that each couple bears the brunt of entertaining (cleaning the house, setting up for the party, and making a salad or side dish and dessert) only once a season. As Hope Murphy explains it, "What I love most about these soup-swap suppers is that we all *own* this event. The soup suppers belong to us all, not solely to me or to whomever is hosting that evening."

THE BASICS OF HOSTING A SOUP SWAP

Soup-swap suppers are simple. You can mix it up and create your own supper, but here is how ours works. Use this rundown as a guideline to create your own.

Every month the dinner is held at the home of a different family. The hosts provide a side dish (almost always a salad of some sort to keep the meal light and simple); bread (store-bought or homemade) or biscuits or corn bread; and dessert (again, very simple; think fruit, cookies, pie, or brownies). Guests bring a pot of soup along with empty take-out and plastic containers with tight-fitting lids for the leftovers they will bring home at the end of the evening. You can coordinate the menu, but in our group we never talk about what we are making ahead of the party, and we never once have had duplicate soups!

How many people should you include? You can heat only four soups at a time (six to eight if you have an oversize stove top), so you don't want to invite too many people (and have to deal with too many pots of soup). Because we live in northern New England, we often use woodstoves—even fireplaces—to reheat soup when we have an over-abundance. You can also use a portable burner or outdoor gas grill, depending on what part of

the country you live in. Or if you want to have a big soup-swap party, think about heating half of the lighter soups first, swapping pots, and then reheating the remaining soups. Soup swaps work with two people or twenty; it's entirely up to you.

Be sure to give a week or two's notice to all the participants, so that they have enough time to plan what soup they want to make and to make it as delicious as possible.

What Should We Bring?

Ask everyone to bring a pot of soup, containers for leftovers, and a ladle to serve the soup. It became clear, very quickly on, that most ladles look exactly alike, so we started putting colored string or tape with our names on the end of ours to keep them separate. Generally the hosts provide spoons, bowls, napkins, forks, and plates if needed.

It's really important to think your recipe through and bring *everything* you'll need for your soup. Relying on your host/hostess to have the necessary equipment at the last minute is not a good idea. If you're going to grate cheese into a finished soup, grate the cheese at home or bring the cheese *and* a grater. If you need to chop herbs at the last minute, bring a small chopping board and a knife. It can be overwhelming when everyone arrives needing kitchen equipment.

Portions

Be sure to pace yourself by sampling only a small portion of each soup. You want to taste them all without getting too full. (I, embarrassingly, always manage to taste all the soups without getting full, but there are some in our group who always complain of filling up too quickly on the first couple of soups they try!)

All the recipes in this book serve six to eight people, some a bit more, some a little less. But remember, you won't be eating full portions of any one soup (unless someone goes crazy and falls in love with one), so there should be enough to serve anywhere from ten to sixteen tasting portions and six to eight full portions. Generally, a tasting portion is around ½ cup [120 ml], and a full-size portion is about 1 cup [240 ml] of soup. The reason these measurements are not precise is that some of these soups are very rich and filling, so you'll want even less than what I've suggested, and others are light, so you might prefer a bigger portion. The suggested serving size is only a guideline.

And many of the cooks in my soup swap simply double the recipe they make, so there is one pot for the party and one pot exclusively for take-home leftovers. Two smaller pots of soup (rather than one huge pot) make sense; you can reheat one for the party and save the other one for the end of the night, when it becomes time to divvy up the leftovers. The take-home soup doesn't need to be hot; in fact, it's much easier to ladle room-temperature soup into containers than it is to ladle boiling-hot soup. For the most part, soup recipes are very forgiving; all the recipes in this book can be doubled.

The Recipes

Here is a key to the symbols that you'll see in the recipes. These will make it easy to quickly find an appropriate recipe for those on the most typical restricted diets.

C = Can be served cold

DF = Dairy-free

GF = Gluten-free

V = Vegetarian

VG = Vegan

The Setup

Logistics are important when it comes to feeding a group of people, and not everyone has a large eat-in kitchen or formal-size dining room. Organization is key.

HEAT IT UP

Remove everything from your stove-top burners to make room for the soup pots. If you have a woodstove, you can use it for any extras. I recommend serving four soups at a time (or six, depending on how many burners you have on your stove top). Heat them until hot, serve, and then heat up the remaining soups. If you need a burner for reheating a topping, be sure to let the host or hostess know ahead of time. Burner space is precious at soup swaps. It's best to prepare toppings at home or to reheat them in the oven.

TOPPINGS

Set up all the toppings—bowls of grated cheese, pesto, chopped scallions, crème fraîche, etc.—on a counter or small table near the stove so that everyone can find them easily. You can have each guest explain which topping pairs with his or her soup as part of the soup introduction. For larger parties, indicate which soup goes with each topping on a small index card and place it in front of the appropriate topping. We never serve soups in any particular order. Not everyone has to taste the same soup at the same time. Each of the topping recipes makes enough for eight people to sprinkle some onto their soup. If you have a large crowd, you may want to double the recipes.

BOWLS

The host sets out bowls and spoons. A word on bowls: You want small bowls, mugs, or ½-cup [120-ml] ramekins. Tasting four, five, or six different soups is incredibly filling, so you really just want a tasting portion as opposed to a big, deep, main-course-size bowlful. The vessels don't need to match; an eclectic collection looks great.

SIDE DISHES

Heavy hors d'oeuvres are not necessary; soups are very filling. A small cheese platter, some crackers, olives, crudités—remember, the soup should be the star! Keep side dishes light and simple; salad or warm roasted vegetables with a loaf of crusty bread, depending on the soups that are being served. I've included a whole chapter of side dishes to get you started. Set out salad plates (for side dishes and bread) and forks.

Choose a Soup That Travels Well

Almost every single one of the soups offered here travels well (save the ones that don't for when it's your turn to host). Look at the end of the recipe for the *To Go* section, which offers tips on the best way to prepare a soup for travel. For instance, it's best not to add last-minute toppings or pasta (which can get overcooked and mushy) before arriving at the party. Generally, the less work you have to do at the party, the better. Keep it simple. For tips on how to keep the lid attached to your soup pot and other advice based on our experience, see "No Spills" on the facing page.

No Spills

Bungee cords or oversize rubber bands (the kind the post office uses to wrap your mail when there's a particularly large amount) are great for keeping lids attached to pots of hot soup when you are transporting them to a soup party. Take one small bungee cord and attach it to the left pot handle, then pull it across the lid and attach to the right side of the pot. Use a second bungee cord or rubber band and repeat, working from the right side. You also might want to wrap the cord around the lid and the soup pot, or through the lid and soup pot handles to keep it in place.

We live in a rural area, so we are always packing pots of soup in the car and traveling to one another's homes. If you live in the city and will be walking or taking the subway, you might want to do the same and wrap the soup in several tea towels to prevent spilling it or burning your hands. Or place your hot soup pot (with the bungee cords securing the lid) in a large tote bag or insulated bag for travel.

Drinks

Beverages are up to you. Many of us arrive with a bottle of wine. One member of our Soup Swap group is a master brewer, and he always brings a collection of his own beer. Seltzer? Soda? Hard or regular cider? Juice? You can ask the host to provide soft drinks, coffee, and tea, and have all the guests bring a bottle of whatever else they would like to drink. We found that soup goes incredibly well with both red and white wine, beer, and hard cider.

Recipes

I've found that people always want the recipe if they particularly like a certain soup. So, ask everyone to e-mail or print out his or her soup recipe to share with the group.

Themes

We never have themes, because we love the spontaneous way the meal just comes together. I've spoken to others in soup groups who divide up the soups—"You do an Asian-inspired soup, and I'll do something Mediterranean." The only "theme" we ever tried was gender related. After realizing that it was primarily the women who were doing the cooking, the men stepped up and agreed to cook for the following party. The results were very impressive. There are lots of ways to create a theme. Have the group choose a soup from among their favorites; it could be as straightforward as a chicken soup or a soup from childhood, a vegetable soup based on what's in season, a soup that was inspired by a trip to a foreign locale, or a soup that is related in some way to each person's background or cultural identity.

Instead of taking home leftovers, maybe you want to think about donating them to a local soup kitchen or a family in need. Just another way of letting the warmth and comfort of soup go a bit further in the community.

Leftovers and Packing It Up to Go

You can use mason jars, leftover plastic yogurt containers, take-out containers, or even zip-tight plastic bags. Be sure not to overfill your containers; about three-fourths full is best if you plan on freezing soup. Make sure you have a tightly sealed, covered container so that when you travel home and put the soup in the refrigerator or freezer it is protected. Some people like to bring clean tea towels or old hand towels to wrap glass jars so they don't knock against one another in their tote bags.

LABELS

Be sure to bring masking tape or canning labels to identify the type of soup and the date it was prepared. This will help you to keep track of it in your freezer. It could be a slight disappointment to think you're thawing a chicken noodle soup only to find out that it's actually cream of mushroom.

How Long Will the Soups Last?

All these soups and stocks should be stored in a tightly sealed glass jar, plastic container, or zip-tight plastic bag. They can be kept in the refrigerator for about four days, or in the freezer for up to four months. Freezing soups with a lot of dairy—like chowders and cream-filled soups—isn't a great idea. Try to consume them within a few days or omit the dairy until the soup is thawed and reheated. Each recipe gives specific instructions for storage.

THE FOUNDATION: MAKING BROTHS & STOCKS

Homemade stock—two scary words? Not really. Try one of these recipes and see just how simple it is to make stock at home. Add poultry, meat, or fish to a big pot with a few vegetables (or leave out the meat and add extra vegetables) and aromatics; add enough water to barely cover; and . . . walk away. An hour or so later you've got stock. Not so scary after all; is it?

The recipes here include classics— chicken stock, beef stock, and fish stock— as well as a really creative technique for using leftover vegetable scraps and chicken, lamb, and beef bones (the stuff you would normally throw away) to create rich, full-flavored stocks.

Remember, when you make your own stock *you* control the amount of salt you use. That's not something you can say about boxed and canned stocks that are generally loaded with sodium and preservatives.

Why Aren't There Specific Amounts of Salt and Pepper Called for in These Recipes?

Sure, I could tell you how much salt to add to each of these soup recipes. But I don't know if you're working with a canned or boxed stock that is loaded with sodium or with a low-sodium variety. And you'll need a lot less salt if you're using one of the homemade stock recipes.

The amount of salt and pepper you add to a soup is a very personal decision. When I say, "Season with salt and pepper," I mean it quite literally. Add salt (and pepper, when called for) to a recipe in several stages and taste after each time you add it. Don't add more until the end of the recipe, when you can see how all the flavors come together and how much more seasoning is really needed. It's easy to add more salt or pepper, but there is no way to add less. Always steer toward less, knowing that you can adjust/add the salt and pepper before serving.

A word about salt: I like to use sea salt. I find that it offers a fuller flavor than processed salts, so less is needed. It's not necessary to go out and buy an expensive bag of fancy sea salt. If you choose to use kosher salt (another good choice), you'll need even less than sea salt, because kosher salt has larger and lighter crystals.

A word about pepper: If you don't have a pepper grinder, it's an investment (albeit a small one) you owe yourself. Grinding fresh peppercorns makes a world of difference in cooking. Cooking with preground black pepper is like using black sawdust. At the very least, buy peppercorns that come packaged in a rudimentary but serviceable grinder, now available in most supermarkets.

PEA BROTH

MAKES ABOUT 8 CUPS [2 L]

The time to make this sweet pea broth is late spring/early summer, when fresh peas are plentiful. As you shell peas for soup or salad, be sure to keep the shells to make this broth. It offers an exceptionally pure, subtly sweet flavor. This broth is the base of Late-Spring Pea and Lettuce Soup (page 53), but it can be used as a vegetable broth in virtually any recipe.

4 lb [1.8 kg] shells from shelling peas (also called English peas) or from sugar snap peas

1 onion, chopped

Dark green leaves from 1 large leek (optional)

6 peppercorns

½ cup [30 g] packed chopped fresh parsley with stems

⅓ cup [20 g] packed chopped fresh chives

Sea salt

Freshly ground black pepper

1. In a large stockpot, combine the pea shells, onion, leek leaves (if using), peppercorns, parsley, and chives and season with salt. Add enough cold water to just barely cover and bring to a boil over high heat. Turn the heat to low, cover, and simmer for 45 minutes to 1 hour. Taste the broth. If the flavor is weak, remove the lid and simmer over medium heat for another 15 minutes, or until the flavors have bloomed. Taste and adjust the seasoning, adding pepper and more salt if needed. Strain the stock, pressing down on the pea shells to release all the juice, and let cool.

2. Store in airtight containers in the refrigerator for up to 5 days or in the freezer for up to 4 months.

RICH BEEF-BONE BROTH

MAKES ABOUT 10 CUPS [2.4 L]

Beef-bone broth has become all the rage in recent years, due to the popularity of the Paleo diet, one that promotes eating lots of meat as well as this type of rich, nourishing broth. It is said to have all kinds of health benefits, since it's rich in protein, gelatin, and anti-oxidants.

You can sip it as a protein-rich snack or meal all on its own or you can strain the broth, discard all the vegetables (the meat should be tender and still full of flavor), and use it as a base for any meat soup. For drinking the broth on its own, cook it for the full 3 hours. If you are using it as a base for other soups, particularly Late-Fall Vegetable Ramen in Miso-Ginger Broth (page 40) or Russian-Style Beef Borscht (page 126), simmer it for 1 to 1½ hours to avoid overcooking the meat, which you'll be adding to the soup.

2 lb [910 g] beef shanks
2½ lb [1.2 kg] short ribs with bones
1 Tbsp olive oil
1½ Tbsp tomato paste
Sea salt
Freshly ground black pepper
1 large onion, quartered
2 medium carrots, peeled and coarsely chopped
2 large celery stalks, coarsely chopped
¼ cup [60 ml] apple cider vinegar
½ cup [30 g] packed chopped fresh parsley
1 bay leaf
6 black peppercorns
4 garlic cloves, peeled and left whole

1. Position a rack in the middle of the oven and preheat to 425°F [220°C].

2. In a large shallow roasting pan, combine the beef shanks and short ribs. Coat both sides of the meat with the olive oil and tomato paste and season with salt and ground pepper. Add the onion, carrots, and celery. Roast for 15 minutes, flip the bones and vegetables, and roast for another 45 minutes. (The goal is not to cook the meat completely but to brown the bones enough to give the broth a rich, deep color.) Remove the pan from the oven and deglaze with the vinegar, scraping up any bits clinging to the bottom of the pan.

3. In a large stockpot, combine the roasted bones and vegetables, the pan juices, parsley, bay leaf, peppercorns, and garlic and season with salt. Add enough cold water to just barely cover and bring to a boil over high heat. Turn the heat to low and simmer, uncovered, for 45 minutes. Partially cover the pot and simmer for another 1 to 3 hours (see headnote), or until the stock has a rich, full flavor. Taste and adjust the seasoning, adding more salt and ground pepper if needed.

4. The stock will be quite fatty. The best way to deal with this is to chill it for several hours (or preferably overnight) and remove the layer of hardened fat from the top with a large kitchen spoon. Then reheat the broth, strain it, and let cool. The meat will be exceptionally tender; reserve it for soups and salads.

5. Store in airtight containers in the refrigerator for up to 5 days or in the freezer for up to 4 months.

Skimming the Fat, Storing the Stock

When you make homemade stock there's always a layer of fat on top that can be difficult to remove when the soup is hot or even warm. The solution? Chill out. Leave yourself time to place the stock in the freezer for an hour or so, or in the refrigerator for several hours (preferably overnight), so that the fat will rise to the top, chill, and harden. (On cold winter days I will put the stockpot outside in the snow, safely covered, to chill.) Use a large kitchen spoon to skim off the hardened fat. Then you can transfer the cooled stock to jars, plastic containers, or well-sealed plastic bags for freezing.

Never fill a container more than three-fourths full because, when frozen, stocks expand. Stocks will last, covered, in the refrigerator for about 5 days. They will last in the freezer for up to 4 months. You can also fill an ice-cube tray with the cooled stock and freeze it. Once frozen, pop the cubes out and store them in a tightly sealed plastic bag for up to 6 months. That way you can have a little stock— or a lot—as needed.

BASIC BEEF STOCK

MAKES ABOUT 8 CUPS [2 L]

This is a straightforward beef stock made from marrow, knuckle, and/or shin beef bones. If you want an extra-rich flavor, you can roast the bones and vegetables in a large roasting pan in a 450°F [230°C] oven for 30 minutes before placing in a stockpot with water. Plan on making the stock a day ahead so it has time to chill overnight, an important step that will enable you to remove the layer of fat that will form on top (see "Skimming the Fat, Storing the Stock," facing page).

4 lb [1.8 kg] beef bones, such as marrow, knuckles, and/or shin bones

2 large carrots, peeled and chopped

2 large celery stalks with leaves, chopped

1 large onion, quartered

6 peppercorns

1 bay leaf

¼ cup [15 g] chopped fresh parsley

Sea salt

1. In a large stockpot, combine the beef bones, carrots, celery, onion, peppercorns, bay leaf, and parsley and season with salt. Add enough cold water to just barely cover and bring to a boil over high heat. Turn the heat to low, partially cover, and simmer for about 2 hours. If fat forms on the surface, skim it off and stir the stock a few times. Taste the stock. If the flavor is weak, remove the lid, and simmer over medium heat for another 10 to 15 minutes, or until flavorful. Strain the stock (be sure to eat that delicious marrow inside the bones, served with a sprinkling of good sea salt, maybe even spread on thinly sliced toast) and let cool overnight in the pot, then remove the layer of fat.

2. Store in airtight containers in the refrigerator for up to 5 days or in the freezer for up to 4 months.

"RECYCLED" LAMB STOCK

MAKES ABOUT 8 CUPS [2 L]

This is a delicious stock that's easy to make after you've roasted a leg of lamb or braised or roasted lamb ribs or lamb shoulder. You can even use the leftover bones from a rack of lamb or lamb chops. The stock can be used as a substitute for beef stock (if you want a subtle lamb flavor in your soup).

1 bone from a roasted leg of lamb, or bones from lamb ribs, lamb shoulder, or 8 lamb rib chops (about 2 lb [910 g])

1 large onion, quartered

1 large carrot, peeled and chopped

2 large celery stalks with leaves, chopped

½ cup [30 g] packed chopped fresh parsley

8 peppercorns

1 bay leaf

Sea salt

Freshly ground black pepper

1. In a large stockpot, combine the lamb bone(s), onion, carrot, celery, parsley, peppercorns, and bay leaf and season with salt and ground pepper. Add enough cold water to just barely cover and bring to a boil over high heat. Turn the heat to low, partially cover, and simmer for about 1½ hours, or until the stock is flavorful. Taste the stock. If the flavor is weak, remove the lid and simmer over medium heat for another 10 to 15 minutes. Taste and adjust the seasoning, adding more salt and ground pepper if needed. Strain the stock and let cool.

2. Store in airtight containers in the refrigerator for up to 5 days or in the freezer for up to 4 months.

BASIC CHICKEN STOCK

MAKES 8 TO 10 CUPS [2 TO 2.4 L]

This simple chicken stock is the backbone of many great soups; it asks very little of you but it gives you so much flavor. Making chicken stock is easy, and you wind up with a pot of gorgeous stock as well as a fully cooked chicken, which you can use in soups, tacos, salads, potpies, and more. Be sure to freeze any leftovers so you're ready to make soup with homemade stock on a moment's notice.

One 4-lb [1.8-kg] roasting chicken or 4 lb [1.8 kg] chicken backs and necks

1 large onion, quartered

4 medium carrots, peeled and cut crosswise into 1-in [2.5-cm] pieces

2 large celery stalks, cut crosswise into 1-in [2.5-cm] pieces

1 large parsnip, peeled and cut crosswise into 1-in [2.5-cm] pieces (optional)

½ cup [30 g] packed chopped fresh parsley

1 bay leaf

6 black peppercorns

Sea salt

Freshly ground black pepper

1. In a large stockpot, combine the chicken, onion, carrots, celery, parsnip (if using), parsley, bay leaf, and peppercorns and season with salt. Add enough cold water to just barely cover and bring to a boil over high heat. Turn the heat to low, partially cover, and simmer for about 1 hour, or until the chicken is quite tender and the stock is flavorful. Taste the stock. If the flavor is weak, remove the lid and simmer over medium heat for another 15 to 30 minutes. Taste and adjust the seasoning, adding more salt and ground pepper if needed.

2. With a slotted spoon, remove the chicken, allowing any stock to drain back into the pot. You can reserve the chicken and use the meat for other dishes. (The chicken meat will keep tightly wrapped in aluminum foil or plastic wrap in the refrigerator for up to 3 days.) Strain the stock and let cool.

3. Store in airtight containers in the refrigerator for up to 5 days or in the freezer for up to 4 months.

ROASTED CHICKEN STOCK

MAKES 8 TO 10 CUPS [2 TO 2.4 L]

Although there are two steps involved in making this stock (roasting the bird and vegetables and then simmering them in a pot of water), it comes with two distinct advantages. The first is a stock that is rich, deeply colored, and full of roasted flavor. The second? The chicken, which will have a firmer texture than that of traditional boiled chicken, can then be used in soups. I especially like to use it in Sopa de Lima (page 87). And be sure to skim some of the fat off the top and save it (in the refrigerator for several days or in the freezer for up to 3 months) for matzo balls (see page 92).

One 4-lb [1.8-kg] roasting chicken or about 4 lb [1.8 kg] chicken backs and necks

3 carrots, peeled and chopped

1 large onion, quartered

1 Tbsp olive oil

Sea salt

Freshly ground black pepper

6 black peppercorns

1 bay leaf

½ cup [30 g] packed chopped fresh parsley

2 large celery stalks with leaves, chopped

1. Position a rack in the middle of the oven and preheat to 450°F [230°C].

2. In a large roasting pan big enough to hold the whole chicken without crowding, arrange the chicken, carrots, and onion; drizzle with the olive oil; and season with salt and ground pepper. Roast for 30 minutes, or until the skin on the chicken is golden brown.

3. In a large stockpot, combine the roasted chicken, carrots, and onion with the peppercorns, bay leaf, parsley, and celery and season with salt and ground pepper. Add enough cold water to just barely cover and bring to a boil over high heat. Turn the heat to low, partially cover, and simmer for about 1 hour, or until the stock is flavorful. Taste the stock. If the flavor is weak, remove the lid and simmer over medium heat for another 15 to 30 minutes. Taste and adjust the seasoning, adding more salt and ground pepper if needed.

4. With a slotted spoon, remove the chicken, allowing any stock to drain back into the pot. You can reserve the chicken and use the meat for other dishes. (The chicken meat will keep tightly wrapped in aluminum foil or plastic wrap in the refrigerator for up to 3 days.) Strain the stock and let cool.

5. Store in airtight containers in the refrigerator for up to 5 days or in the freezer for up to 4 months.

"RECYCLED" CHICKEN OR TURKEY STOCK

MAKES 8 TO 10 CUPS [2 TO 2.4 L]

For classic chicken stock, you simmer a raw bird and vegetables for hours. For this easy version, you "recycle" the carcass from a roasted chicken or turkey and add fresh vegetables. You won't believe how much rich flavor you can coax from a leftover chicken or turkey carcass. If you have a large bird you can make this stock with one carcass, but you will have a much richer, more flavorful stock if you use two. Remove any big pieces of leftover meat to use in soups, salads, and sandwiches. And be sure to skim some of the fat off the top and save it (in the refrigerator for several days or in the freezer for up to 3 months) for making matzo balls (see page 92).

1 large leek
1 to 2 roasted chicken carcasses or 1 turkey carcass
3 onions, chopped
6 celery stalks with leaves, chopped
4 carrots, peeled and chopped
1 cup [60 g] packed chopped fresh parsley
2 bay leaves
8 black peppercorns
Sea salt
Freshly ground black pepper

||||||||||||||||||||||||||||||||||

1. Halve the leek lengthwise. Rinse under cold running water, pat dry, and coarsely chop.

2. In a large stockpot, combine the chicken carcass(es), leek, onions, celery, carrots, parsley, bay leaves, and peppercorns and season with salt. Add enough cold water to just barely cover and bring to a boil over high heat. Turn the heat to low, partially cover, and simmer for about 1 hour. If fat forms on the surface, skim it off and stir the stock a few times. Taste the stock. If the flavor is weak, remove the lid and simmer over medium heat for another 15 to 30 minutes, or until flavorful. Taste and adjust the seasoning, adding ground pepper and more salt if needed. Strain the stock and let cool.

3. Store in airtight containers in the refrigerator for up to 5 days or in the freezer for up to 4 months.

Do I Really *Need* to Make Homemade Stock?

Get real. We're busy people. We have places to go, people to see, things to get done. And soup, well it takes time. So do we really need to complicate matters by having to make our own stock?

Well, not so fast. The thing is, you can make perfectly delicious soup using boxed stock (look for organic, low-sodium varieties). It will be full of flavor and make you feel good. Unfortunately, no matter which brand you use, it may also be loaded with sodium and a few unwanted ingredients (like preservatives and artificial flavorings).

Putting a chicken (or beef or fish bones) in a pot with a few vegetables, covering them with water, and letting the mixture simmer for an hour or so *unattended* isn't really a huge commitment. Does the flavor pay off? Is it worth "giving up" that hour? The answer is unequivocally Yes! And when you make your own stock, you can control exactly how much salt or pepper goes into your soup as well as the balance of the final flavor.

When I make stock (which I like to do once or twice a month or when I have lots of leftovers or need a cooked chicken) I always make a big pot or two (more than I'll need for one soup) and freeze the leftovers so I can make a quick soup with homemade stock at a moment's notice.

Whenever people ask me if making stock from scratch is "worth it," I recall something Julia Child once told me. Yes, *that* Julia Child. While I was interviewing her for a food magazine back in 1978, I asked her if she thought people would ever go back to eating frozen vegetables. "Once you've tasted fresh," she told me in her distinct singsong New England voice, "there's no going back." I've thought about that simple statement many times over the years. Once you make homemade stock and see how ridiculously easy it is, and how much *richer* the flavor is, well "there's no going back."

FISH STOCK

DF GF

MAKES ABOUT 8 CUPS [2 L]

Fish stock, or what the French call *fume*, is quick and easy to make. Ask your local fish store to save you "frames," the bones that are left after filleting a fish. Look for mild-tasting white fish like flounder, cod, halibut, or haddock. Stronger fish like salmon, bluefish, or mackerel are too oily to make a clean-tasting fish stock. You can also add lobster shells to the stockpot.

This stock is the base of many fish soups and chowders. If you don't want to make your own fish stock, ask the folks at your fish store if they make/sell it. It will be much more flavorful than what you find in the supermarket.

4 lb [1.8 kg] fish frames (bones), with or without heads, gills removed (you may need to coarsely chop the bones to fit in your stockpot)

¾ cup [180 ml] dry white wine

1 large onion, quartered

2 medium carrots, peeled and chopped

2 celery stalks, chopped

1 bay leaf

8 peppercorns

½ cup [30 g] packed chopped fresh parsley

6 sprigs fresh thyme or 1 tsp dried

Sea salt

Freshly ground black pepper

1. In a large stockpot, combine the fish bones and wine. Add enough cold water to just barely cover and bring to a boil over high heat. Skim off the white foam that forms on the surface and turn the heat to low. Add the onion, carrots, celery, bay leaf, peppercorns, parsley, and thyme and season with salt (go easy; you can always add more at the end). Partially cover and simmer gently (try not to let it boil or simmer too vigorously) for 20 to 45 minutes. Taste the stock (it should have a mild briny flavor) and adjust the seasoning, adding ground pepper and more salt if needed. (Remember that a lot of sea-food, particularly crustaceans, are salty, so you want to avoid oversalting the stock.) Strain the stock and let cool.

2. Store in airtight containers in the refrigerator for up to 5 days or in the freezer for up to 4 months.

VEGETABLE STOCK

MAKES 8 TO 10 CUPS [2 TO 2.4 L]

The first time I made my own vegetable stock, using scraps I had in the refrigerator, I was amazed at the depth of flavor I got from food I would have otherwise thrown away or composted. This stock takes about an hour and is *so* superior to supermarket canned broth that you'll be hooked.

Start a bag collecting vegetable scraps—think peelings, trimmings, leaves, stems, and more. When you have about 3 lb [1.4 kg], you're ready to make stock. The secret to drawing out the best flavor is *balance*. If you add 3 cups [210 g] of cauliflower or Brussels sprouts trimmings, your broth will have a heavy *brassica* taste; you want to balance members of the onion family with other vegetables such as carrots, celery, fennel, herbs, or mushrooms.

3 to 4 lb [1.4 to 1.8 kg] leftover vegetable scraps, thoroughly washed and chopped

2 carrots, chopped

2 large celery stalks, chopped

6 black peppercorns

1 bay leaf

½ cup [30 g] chopped fresh parsley

Sea salt

1. In a large stockpot, combine all the vegetable scraps, the carrots, celery, peppercorns, bay leaf, and parsley and season with salt. Add enough cold water to just barely cover and bring to a boil over high heat. Turn the heat to low, partially cover, and simmer for about 1 hour, or until the stock is flavorful. Taste the stock. If the flavor is weak, remove the lid and simmer over medium heat for another 10 to 15 minutes. Taste and adjust the seasoning, adding more salt if needed. Strain the stock and let cool.

2. Store in airtight containers in the refrigerator for up to 5 days or in the freezer for up to 4 months.

DASHI

MAKES 10 CUPS [2.4 L]

This is a light, umami-rich stock made from soaking dried seaweed and dried bonito (fish flakes). It's best if you can let the stock soak overnight, but it will be fine after a few hours. You can find dried kelp and bonito flakes at natural food and Japanese food shops.

10 cups [2.4 L] water
2¼ oz [65 g] dried kelp, nori, kombu, or any type of dried seaweed
3 oz [90 g] dried bonito (fish) flakes

1. In a large saucepan over high heat, bring the water to a boil. Turn the heat to low and let simmer. In a large bowl, combine the dried kelp and bonito flakes, add the water, and set aside to soak for at least 4 hours, or up to overnight. Strain the stock through a fine-mesh sieve, pressing down very gently to release all the liquid. Set aside to cool.

2. Store in airtight containers in the refrigerator for up to 5 days or in the freezer for up to 4 months.

VEGETABLE SOUPS

I'm not a vegetarian, but I find this collection of recipes—from the "No-Cream" Cream of Celery Root Soup with Fried Capers to the Tomato Soup with Grilled-Cheese Croutons— among the most exciting in the book. Vegetable soups can be thick and chunky or smooth and puréed. Several of these soups call for vegetables that are roasted at a high temperature, a very interesting technique that gives soup a rich, caramelized flavor. Follow the seasons, and you'll discover vegetable soups to make year-round.

A note to non-vegetarians: Any of the soups in this chapter can be made using chicken stock or beef broth instead of vegetable stock.

JOE'S SUMMER GARDEN TOMATO GAZPACHO

MAKES 10 TO 12 TASTING PORTIONS OR 6 TO 8 FULL SERVINGS

This is my adaptation of my friend Joe Yonan's fabulous gazpacho. As a gardener, not to mention the Food and Dining editor of the *Washington Post*, Joe knows tomatoes.

"Unless you're roasting the tomatoes first to concentrate their flavor," he writes, "you may have to help them taste like themselves. When it's too hot to cook and you want to use raw tomatoes and your blender, you need to add just a touch of vinegar and a little honey or sugar to bring out all their goodness, something like wearing makeup designed to make you look as if you're not wearing makeup."

Stale bread means one- or two-day-old bread that is beginning to turn crusty and hard. If the bread is too hard to cube, place it in a warm (275°F [135°C]) oven for a few minutes to soften it up.

I don't peel the tomatoes, but if you dislike tomato peels, score a small X in the bottom of each tomato and submerge them in a pot of boiling water for 1 minute. Then, using a slotted spoon, remove them from the pot and peel.

6 lb [2.7 kg] ripe tomatoes, cored and chopped

3 to 4 garlic cloves, chopped

2 cups [65 g] ½-in [12-mm] stale bread cubes

20 large basil leaves

8 scallions

1 medium Vidalia onion, chopped

1 medium sweet green or red bell pepper, chopped

1 medium cucumber, peeled and chopped

6 Tbsp [90 ml] olive oil, plus more as needed

6 Tbsp [90 ml] apple cider vinegar, plus more as needed

2 tsp mild honey, plus more as needed

Sea salt

Freshly ground black pepper

GARNISHES

12 cherry tomatoes or 2 medium tomatoes, chopped

1 medium peeled cucumber, chopped

1 large red or green bell pepper, chopped

4 scallions, chopped

Polenta Croutons (page 169)

Basil leaves, whole or coarsely chopped

1. In a large bowl, combine the summer tomatoes, garlic, bread cubes, basil, scallions, onion, bell pepper, cucumber, olive oil, vinegar, and honey; season with salt and pepper. Using a food processor or blender and working in batches, purée the mixture until almost smooth. The soup will be chunky. If the soup is too thick, add more oil and vinegar and purée it a bit longer. Taste and adjust the seasoning, adding more salt, pepper, and honey if needed. Cover and refrigerate for about 2 hours.

2. Ladle the soup into mugs or bowls and serve cold, topped with any or all of the garnishes.

TO GO: Pack up the garnishes in separate containers.

LATE-FALL VEGETABLE RAMEN IN MISO-GINGER BROTH

DF · **V** · **VG**

MAKES 8 TO 10 TASTING PORTIONS OR 6 FULL SERVINGS

This is a *very* simplified version of ramen, the classic Japanese noodle soup. While you simmer a variety of late-fall vegetables in a miso-and-ginger–flavored broth, you cook the ramen noodles. To serve, you can top each bowl with crunchy slices of sunchokes (Jerusalem artichokes) and spicy mustard greens if you want to make your ramen even more interesting. This broth is serious comfort food, perfect for a sore throat or for when you're feeling down. I love ginger, and the more the merrier. This is a strong ginger statement, so feel free to use the smaller amount if you're not crazy about the rhizome. This also tastes really great with chicken stock instead of vegetable broth.

1 Tbsp canola oil

1½ oz [40 g] fresh ginger, peeled; half chopped and half cut into thin matchsticks

3 scallions, finely chopped

2 medium carrots, peeled and cut on the diagonal into ½-in [12-mm] pieces

9½ oz [270 g] seeded, peeled fall squash, such as butternut, cut into ½-in [12-mm] cubes

Freshly ground black pepper

2½ Tbsp white miso paste

½ tsp chili oil, sesame chili oil, or hot-pepper sauce

1 Tbsp soy sauce

6 cups [1.4 L] Vegetable Stock (page 34) or canned low-sodium broth

14 oz [400 g] udon or ramen wheat noodles

1 cup [230 g] peeled, thinly sliced sunchokes or sliced water chestnuts (optional)

½ cup [30 g] packed chopped mustard greens or other spicy fresh greens (optional)

1. In a large stockpot over low heat, warm the canola oil. Add all the ginger and half the scallions and cook, stirring, for 3 minutes. Add the carrots and squash, season with pepper, and cook, stirring, for another 3 minutes. Add the miso paste and stir until the vegetables are well coated, then add the chili oil, soy sauce, and vegetable stock. Turn the heat to high and bring to a boil. Turn the heat to low, partially cover, and simmer for 15 to 20 minutes, or until the vegetables are just tender.

2. Meanwhile bring a large pot of water to a boil over high heat. Add the noodles and boil them for about 3 minutes, or until just tender. Transfer the noodles to a colander and drain.

3. Divide the noodles among mugs or bowls and top with equal portions of broth and vegetables. Top with the remaining scallions and the sunchokes and mustard greens, if desired, and serve.

TO GO: Boil the noodles at home but cook them for only 2 minutes. Drain them and let cool. Pack the noodles with about ⅓ cup [80 ml] of the cooking liquids (so they don't clump up and stick together) in a covered container. Pack the sunchokes and mustard greens separately. Reheat the soup at the party. Be sure to drain the noodles before adding to the hot soup, where they will finish cooking.

PARSNIP AND CAULIFLOWER "VICHYSSOISE" WITH GREMOLATA

MAKES 10 TO 12 TASTING PORTIONS OR 8 FULL SERVINGS

The thick, creamy texture of this vegetable soup reminds me of a potato-leek soup, or vichyssoise. Here, the base of the soup is made with cauliflower (instead of potatoes), leeks, and parsnips, which provide a wonderfully earthy flavor. The creamy texture of the soup is offset by the crunchy lemon-and-herb-infused toasted bread crumbs that are sprinkled on top. This soup is delicious cold. Let it come to room temperature, cover, and chill in the refrigerator for about 4 hours. Serve with Crostada with Butternut, Red Onion, and Feta (page 153).

2 medium leeks

1 Tbsp butter

1 Tbsp olive oil

1 medium-large parsnip, peeled and coarsely chopped

1 medium head cauliflower, cut into medium florets

1 tsp chopped fresh thyme

Sea salt

Freshly ground black pepper

7 cups [1.7 L] Vegetable Stock (page 34)

¼ cup [60 ml] heavy cream

Gremolata (page 165) for serving

||||||||||||||||||||||||||||||||||

1. Trim off the dark green sections from the leeks and save for making vegetable stock. Halve the pale green and white sections lengthwise. Rinse under cold running water, pat dry, and cut crosswise into ½-in [12-mm] pieces.

2. In a large stockpot over low heat, melt the butter. Add the olive oil and leeks, cover, and cook for 10 minutes, or until the leeks are tender. Add the parsnip, cauliflower, and thyme and season with salt and pepper. Add the vegetable stock and stir to combine. Turn the heat to medium-high and bring to a boil. Turn the heat to low, cover, and simmer for 30 minutes, or until the parsnip and cauliflower soften. Remove from the heat, remove the lid, and let cool for about 5 minutes.

3. Using a food processor or blender and working in batches or using a handheld immersion blender, purée the soup until smooth. Return the soup to the pot. Stir in the heavy cream. Taste and adjust the seasoning, adding more salt and pepper if needed. Bring to a gentle simmer over low heat.

4. Ladle the soup into mugs or bowls and serve topped with a small spoonful of gremolata.

TO GO: Pack the gremolata separately.

POTATO-LEEK SOUP
WITH CHIVE OIL

C GF V

MAKES 10 TO 12 TASTING PORTIONS OR 8 FULL SERVINGS

This is a classic. Served hot, it's potato-leek soup, one of the best comfort foods around; served cold, it's called vichyssoise and is thoroughly refreshing. If you're serving the soup cold, plan on letting it chill for 4 to 6 hours. The soup and the chive oil can be prepared up to 24 hours ahead. Serve with Mixed Greens Salad with Mint-Tangerine Vinaigrette (page 156).

8 medium leeks

1½ Tbsp olive oil

2 Tbsp minced chives, plus more for garnish

1 Tbsp chopped fresh thyme

5 large medium-starch potatoes, like russets or Yukon gold, peeled and cut into 2-in [5-cm] pieces

8 cups [2 L] Vegetable Stock (page 34) or canned low-sodium broth

Sea salt

Freshly ground black pepper

½ cup plus 2 Tbsp [150 ml] heavy cream

Chive Oil (page 164) for serving

1. Trim off the dark green sections from the leeks and save for making vegetable stock. Halve the pale green and white sections lengthwise. Rinse under cold running water, pat dry, and cut crosswise into 2-in [5-cm] pieces.

2. In a large stockpot over low heat, warm the olive oil. Add the leeks, chives, and thyme; cover; and cook, stirring occasionally, for 10 minutes. Add the potatoes, stir well, and cook for another 2 minutes. Add 7½ cups [1.8 L] of the vegetable stock and season with salt and pepper (if using canned broth, be careful not to over-salt the soup). Turn the heat to high and bring to a boil. Turn the heat to low, cover, and simmer for 15 to 20 minutes, or until the potatoes are tender. Remove from the heat and let cool slightly.

3. Using a food processor or blender and working in batches or using a handheld immersion blender, purée the soup until smooth. Return the soup to the pot. If the soup is too thick, add the remaining ½ cup [120 ml] stock. Add the cream and stir until blended. Taste and adjust the seasoning, adding more salt and pepper if needed. Bring to a simmer over low heat or cover and chill for 4 to 6 hours.

4. Ladle the soup into mugs or bowls and serve, hot or cold, with a generous 1 tsp chive oil swirled into each and a sprinkling of minced chives.

TO GO: If serving chilled, pack the cold soup with ice packs. Pack the chive oil separately.

ASPARAGUS AND LEEK SOUP
WITH POACHED EGG

MAKES 8 TO 10 TASTING PORTIONS OR 8 FULL SERVINGS

Every part of the asparagus is used in a different way to create this spring soup. The tough root ends (which are normally discarded) are simmered with the stock to infuse it with an asparagus flavor. The tender middle section is used to make the "body" of the soup, and the prized delicate tips are sautéed and added to the soup as a garnish.

The soup is excellent on its own, but if you want to add a little more pizzazz, poach some eggs, add one to the center of each bowl of hot soup, and then sprinkle with the sautéed asparagus and scallions. Cutting into the egg and releasing its bright yellow yolk into the green soup produces a dramatic visual effect as well as extra-rich flavor. The soup is also excellent garnished with Polenta Croutons (page 169) and served with Mixed Greens Salad with Mint-Tangerine Vinaigrette (page 156).

2½ lb [910 g] asparagus

1 large leek

7 cups [1.4 L] Vegetable Stock (page 34)

1½ Tbsp olive oil

2½ Tbsp chopped fresh chives

Sea salt

Freshly ground black pepper

¼ cup [60 ml] dry white wine

2 scallions, trimmed, white and green sections very thinly sliced

½ tsp freshly grated lemon zest

1 egg per serving, preferably organic

IIIIIIIIIIIIIIIIIIIIIIIIIIIIIIIII

1. Cut about 2 in [5 cm] off the tough root ends of each asparagus spear; reserve the remaining asparagus. Trim off the dark green section of the leek and coarsely chop. Halve the pale green and white section lengthwise, rinse under cold running water, and pat dry; reserve.

2. In a medium saucepan, combine the tough asparagus ends and the dark green leek pieces. Add the vegetable stock and bring to a boil over medium-high heat. Turn the heat to medium-low, cover, and simmer for about 15 minutes.

3. Meanwhile, cut the tips off the top of the remaining asparagus spears and set aside. Cut the middle sections crosswise into 1-in [2.5-cm] pieces. Cut the pale green and white section of the leek crosswise into thin pieces.

4. In a large stockpot over low heat, warm 1 Tbsp of the olive oil. Add the remaining leek pieces and the chives, season with salt and pepper, and cook, stirring, for 5 minutes. Add the asparagus pieces from the middle of the stalks and cook for another 5 minutes. Turn the heat to high, add the wine, and bring to a boil.

5. Strain the stock from the medium saucepan into the large stockpot (discarding the tough asparagus stems and dark green leek pieces) and return to a boil over high heat. Turn the heat to low, cover, and simmer for 30 minutes. Remove from the heat and let cool for about 5 minutes.

6. Using a food processor or blender and working in batches or using a handheld immersion blender, purée the soup until smooth. Return the soup to the pot. Taste and adjust the seasoning, adding more salt and pepper if needed.

7. In a medium skillet over medium heat, warm the remaining ½ Tbsp olive oil. Add the scallions and cook for 4 minutes, or until they begin to turn a rich golden brown. Add the asparagus tips and lemon zest, season with salt and pepper, and cook, stirring, for about 5 minutes (or for just 2 minutes if reheating later or at the party), or until the asparagus tips are almost tender.

8. Bring a pot of water to a gentle simmer over medium heat. Crack the eggs into the pot, one at a time, and simmer for 3 minutes. With a slotted spoon, carefully transfer the eggs, one at a time, to paper towels to drain. Using a 2-in [5-cm] biscuit cutter or a small sharp knife, cut around each egg white to create a small, perfect circle with just a bit of white.

9. Ladle the soup into mugs or bowls and, using a flat spatula, carefully place a poached egg in the center of each. Sprinkle with some asparagus-tip topping around the egg, avoiding the yolk, and serve.

TO GO: Make the soup as well as the garnish ahead, sautéing the asparagus topping for 2 to 3 minutes, and then pack up the topping separately. Using a slotted spoon, drain the poached eggs before transferring them to a paper towel-lined plastic container large enough to accommodate them in a single layer. When you reheat the soup, it will warm up the garnish as well as the poached egg.

VIETNAMESE-STYLE ASPARAGUS SOUP
WITH NOODLES AND SPICY PEANUT PASTE

MAKES 8 TO 10 TASTING PORTIONS OR 6 FULL SERVINGS

The inspiration for this soup comes from Vietnamese *phô*, a hearty soup of hot chicken stock topped with asparagus and other vegetables, noodles, and a dab of chili paste. A spicy peanut butter–based paste slowly releases its assertive flavor and slightly thickens the broth. All the elements for the soup can be prepared ahead and put together at the very last minute. Chinese chili paste is available at Asian markets and specialty shops and at some supermarkets.

SPICY PEANUT PASTE

3 Tbsp freshly grated or minced fresh peeled ginger

½ tsp Chinese chili paste or hot-pepper sauce

½ cup [150 g] chunky all-natural peanut butter

½ tsp hot chili oil or hot-pepper sauce

2 Tbsp soy sauce

1 tsp toasted Asian sesame oil

3 scallions, finely chopped

SOUP

4 oz [115 g] angel-hair rice noodles

1 Tbsp peanut or vegetable oil

1 tsp toasted Asian sesame oil

½ cup [80 g] julienned peeled fresh ginger

5 scallions, cut on the diagonal into 1½-in [4-cm] pieces

2 lb [910 g] asparagus, ends trimmed, peeled, and cut on the diagonal into 1½-in [4-cm] pieces

6 cups [1.4 L] Vegetable Stock (page 34) or canned low-sodium broth

½ cup [30 g] packed, coarsely chopped fresh cilantro

1 cup [40 g] mung bean sprouts

Coarsely chopped salted peanuts for garnish (optional)

1. **TO MAKE THE PEANUT PASTE:** In a medium bowl, combine the grated ginger, chili paste, and peanut butter, stirring to create a smooth paste. Add the chili oil, soy sauce, sesame oil, and scallions; stir until smooth. The paste will be quite thick and should have a good, spicy kick. The paste can be made several hours ahead; cover and refrigerate until ready to serve.

2. **TO MAKE THE SOUP:** Fill a large bowl with ice water and set aside. Bring a large stockpot of water to a boil over medium heat. Add the rice noodles to the stockpot and cook for about 3 minutes, or until tender. Immediately transfer the noodles to a colander to drain and cool them under very cold running water to stop the cooking. Transfer the noodles to the bowl of ice water and separate them to prevent them from clumping. (If you are good with chopsticks, use them to do this.) Set aside.

continued

3. In a large skillet or wok over medium-high heat, warm the peanut oil and sesame oil. Add the julienned ginger and cook, stirring frequently, for 1 minute. Add the scallions and cook for about 20 seconds. Add the asparagus and cook, stirring frequently, for 3 minutes. The vegetables should be al dente, not completely cooked or soft. Set aside. (The recipe can be made ahead up to this point. Store the noodles and about ¼ cup [60 ml] of the ice water in a separate container and store the sautéed asparagus in plastic wrap. Store all the elements in the refrigerator until ready to assemble. Bring the peanut paste and asparagus to room temperature before finishing off the soup.)

4. In a large stockpot over medium heat, bring the vegetable stock to a rolling boil. Turn the heat to low and keep hot.

5. Ladle ½ to 1 cup [120 to 240 ml] of the simmering stock into each soup bowl and then whisk in about 1 Tbsp of the peanut paste. Drain the noodles well and divide them equally among the bowls. Top each serving with about 1 Tbsp of the asparagus-ginger mixture and sprinkle with a handful of cilantro and bean sprouts. Serve the remaining cilantro, sprouts, spicy peanut paste, and peanuts, if desired, on the side, and let guests add what they like.

TO GO: Transport the vegetable stock in the soup pot. Pack the noodles, the peanut paste, and each of the toppings in separate containers. At the party, reheat the soup and continue as directed. Set out all the toppings so that guests can choose which they want to add.

MISO SOUP
WITH TOFU AND SCALLIONS

MAKES 10 TASTING PORTIONS OR 8 FULL SERVINGS

I've always wondered why no two miso soups taste alike. When it's good it's a satisfying, umami-rich broth, but when it's bad it tastes like warm seaweed water. Real miso soup is made with a Japanese stock called dashi, which is made by soaking dried seaweed and dried bonito (fish) flakes. The dashi is heated and mixed with miso paste, cubes of firm tofu, and very thinly sliced scallions. Miso paste is available in different flavors. The two that work best with this soup are white miso, which has a subtly sweet flavor, and yellow miso, which has a delicate soy flavor. You can also add very fine julienne strips of fresh ginger and any other ingredients you like, but this soup is so delicate and satisfying with just a few ingredients that I recommend keeping it simple. Although traditionally a breakfast soup (better than sugary cereals!), miso is also served as a first course or light addition to any soup supper.

8 cups [2 L] Dashi (page 35)

6 Tbsp [85 g] white or yellow miso paste (see headnote)

One 14-oz [400-g] package firm tofu, cut into ½-in [12-mm] cubes

10 scallions, finely chopped

3 Tbsp very thinly julienned peeled fresh ginger

GARNISHES
Dash of soy sauce or tamari
Chopped fresh cilantro
Julienned fresh carrot
Baby spinach leaves
Cooked shrimp, coarsely chopped or, if small, left whole
Roasted vegetables, cut into ½-in [12-mm] cubes
Shredded cooked chicken

1. In a large stockpot over medium heat, bring the dashi to a simmer. Turn the heat to low and keep hot.

2. In a small bowl, combine the miso paste and about ½ cup [120 ml] of the hot dashi. Using a whisk or the back of a spoon, stir the mixture into a smooth paste. Slowly whisk the miso paste back into the hot dashi and heat for 2 minutes, or until almost simmering. Add the tofu, scallions, and ginger and heat for another 5 minutes, or until gently simmering and hot.

3. Ladle the soup into mugs or bowls and serve hot, topped with any or all of the garnishes.

TO GO: Before adding the tofu, scallions, and ginger, remove the pot from the heat and let cool. Pack the tofu, scallions, and ginger in one container and pack each of the garnishes separately. Before serving, reheat the soup over medium heat until warm; add the tofu, scallions, and ginger; and heat for 5 minutes, or until gently simmering. Serve the hot soup with the garnishes.

HOT-AND-SOUR SOUP

MAKES 8 TO 10 TASTING PORTIONS OR 6 FULL SERVINGS

I adore hot-and-sour soup, but I never thought about making it at home because I believed that it would require too many exotic ingredients and would be terribly time consuming. I was so wrong!

This recipe comes from my friend Grace Young, author of the James Beard Award–winning book *Stir Frying to the Sky's Edge*. The soup doesn't take long and requires only a few Asian ingredients, among them lily buds (a dried botanical that may be labeled "golden needles" or "lily flowers"), which are a traditional ingredient of this soup. But if you can't find them (they're sold in Asian markets), the soup is fine without them.

I have made two changes to Grace's recipe. When I got home from marketing, I realized that I had forgotten to buy canned bamboo shoots, so I used the fresh Jerusalem artichokes (also called sunchokes) I had on hand instead. They turned out to be fabulous crunchy substitutes (as are water chestnuts and jicama). Also, I added a dash of toasted sesame oil for a fuller flavor.

¼ cup [15 g] dried cloud ears (also labeled "tree ears" or "black fungus")

¼ cup [15 g] lily buds (optional but highly recommended)

4 cups [960 ml] Basic Chicken Stock (page 29)

8 oz [230 g] medium-firm tofu, rinsed, patted dry, and cut into ½-in [12-mm] cubes

4 oz [115 g] fresh shiitake mushrooms, stems removed and caps thinly sliced

¼ cup [35 g] canned shredded bamboo shoots, drained and rinsed, or ¼ cup [35 g] peeled and very thinly sliced water chestnuts or jicama

1 Tbsp peeled and finely shredded fresh ginger

2 Tbsp cornstarch

2 Tbsp black rice wine, rice vinegar, or balsamic vinegar, plus more as needed

1 Tbsp soy sauce

1 egg, beaten

2 scallions, trimmed and finely chopped

2 tsp toasted Asian sesame oil, plus more for serving (optional)

½ tsp sugar

½ tsp ground white pepper, plus more as needed

Chili paste for serving (optional)

1. Place the cloud ears and the lily buds in separate bowls, pour about ½ cup [120 ml] cold water over each, and set aside to soak for about 30 minutes. When softened, drain both, discarding the soaking liquid. Remove any hard spots from the cloud ears and cut in half. Remove the hard end from the lily buds and tie them into knots. (Grace says the reason for this is that the Chinese like the look of the tied lily bud because it is more pleasing to the eye. If you don't do it, the lily buds tend to disappear into the soup; the knot gives them texture.)

2. In a 2-qt [2-L] saucepan over high heat, bring the chicken stock to a boil. Add the cloud ears, lily buds, tofu, mushrooms, bamboo shoots, and ginger and return to a boil.

3. Meanwhile, in a small bowl, combine the cornstarch, vinegar, and soy sauce, stirring until the cornstarch has dissolved. When the soup has reached a rolling boil, add the cornstarch mixture and continue boiling, stirring constantly, for 1 to 2 minutes, or until thickened.

4. Remove the pan from the heat and, stirring, add the egg in a thin stream. Add the scallions, sesame oil, sugar, and white pepper; cover; and set aside for about 30 seconds to allow the egg to just set. Taste the soup and adjust the seasoning, adding more vinegar and ground pepper if needed.

5. Ladle the soup into mugs or bowls and serve topped with a tiny drizzle of the toasted sesame oil or chili paste, if desired.

TO GO: Bring some toasted sesame oil or chili paste for those who like extra heat.

LATE-SPRING PEA AND LETTUCE SOUP

C GF V

MAKES 10 TASTING PORTIONS OR 8 FULL SERVINGS

This soup is sweet, light, and bursting with the flavor of fresh spring peas. Look for English peas in local farmers' markets or in the produce section of your favorite supermarket. The pea shells are used to make an incredibly pure, sweet pea broth and then sautéed leeks, peas, chives, and lettuce are added. (Of course, you can also use vegetable or chicken stock.) The soup is then puréed into a gorgeous bright pea-green soup.

You can make the soup a day ahead and reheat it just before serving. The soup can be served hot or cold with a drizzle of heavy cream, crème fraîche, or plain Greek yogurt, and a sprinkling of fresh chives. Polenta Croutons add a welcome texture.

2 medium leeks or 2 large Vidalia onions, chopped

2 heads butter (or butter head) lettuce or Bibb lettuce

3 Tbsp olive oil

Sea salt

Freshly ground black pepper

6 cups [930 g] shelled English peas

⅓ cup [20 g] packed minced fresh chives

8 cups [2 L] Pea Broth (page 23)

Heavy cream, plain Greek yogurt, or crème fraîche for serving (optional)

Polenta Croutons (page 169) for serving (optional)

1. Trim off the dark green sections from the leeks and save for making vegetable stock. Halve the pale green and white sections lengthwise. Rinse under cold running water, pat dry, and cut crosswise into 1-in [2.5-cm] pieces. Core the lettuce, wash thoroughly, and spin dry.

2. In a large stockpot over low heat, warm the olive oil. Add the leeks and season with salt and pepper. Cover the pot and cook, stirring occasionally, for 10 minutes. Add the peas and half of the chives and cook, stirring, for 5 minutes. Add the lettuce and cook for 1 minute more. Turn the heat to high, add the pea broth, and bring to a boil. Turn the heat to low, cover, and simmer for 20 minutes. Taste and adjust the seasoning, adding more salt and pepper if needed. Let cool for about 5 minutes.

3. Using a food processor or blender and working in batches or using a handheld immersion blender, purée the soup until smooth. Return the soup to the pot. If the soup is too thin, turn the heat to medium-high and simmer vigorously until reduced and somewhat thickened. Taste and adjust the seasoning, adding more salt and pepper if needed.

4. Ladle the soup into mugs or bowls. Top each with a dollop of cream and sprinkle with the remaining chives and the croutons, if desired, before serving.

TO GO: Pack the remaining chives and the croutons in separate small containers and bring any dairy you want to add.

SPRING PARSLEY-WATERCRESS SOUP

MAKES 10 TASTING PORTIONS OR 8 FULL SERVINGS

Come spring, the first signs of green show up in many ways—the first blades of grass change color, and the first garden chives pop their heads up through the now softened winter soil. This is a soup/tonic to celebrate a new season. It has the purest spring-green color and a fresh taste that makes you feel instantly invigorated and energized. Top with Fried Parsley or chopped spring chives or both. This soup literally takes about half an hour from start to finish and is surprisingly sophisticated. You can double it to serve a crowd, but one small bowl of this soup is so satisfying that a large main-course-size bowl is really gilding the lily.

There are two ways to serve this soup: as is, which is thick and a touch fibrous, or you can strain the soup through a food mill or a fine-mesh sieve for a texture closer to that of a gorgeous thin parsley broth. Both are delicious, but if you think the fibrous nature of the soup will bother anyone, by all means strain it.

3 Tbsp olive oil

6 scallions, chopped

¼ cup [10 g] packed chopped fresh chives, plus minced chives for garnish (optional)

Sea salt

Freshly ground black pepper

10½ oz [300 g] flat-leaved (Italian) parsley with stems, washed, dried, and chopped

6 oz [170 g] watercress with stems, washed, dried, and chopped

8 cups [2 L] Pea Broth (page 23) or Vegetable Stock (page 34)

Fried Parsley (see page 166) for serving (optional)

1. In a medium stockpot over low heat, warm the olive oil. Add the scallions and chopped chives, season with salt and pepper, and cook, stirring, for 4 minutes. Add the parsley and watercress and cook, stirring occasionally, for 2 minutes. Turn the heat to high, add the pea broth, and bring to a boil. Turn the heat to low, cover, and simmer for 10 minutes. Remove from the heat and let cool for 5 minutes.

2. Using a blender (I have found that food processors and immersion blenders don't purée all the parsley stems properly) and working in batches, purée the soup. Strain the mixture through a fine-meshed strainer if desired and return the soup to the pot. Taste and adjust the seasoning, adding more salt and pepper if needed.

3. Ladle the soup into mugs or bowls and serve hot, garnished with fried parsley or minced chives, if desired.

TO GO: Pack the Fried Parsley and minced chives separately.

"NO-CREAM" CREAM OF CELERY ROOT SOUP
WITH FRIED CAPERS

MAKES 8 TO 10 TASTING PORTIONS OR 6 FULL SERVINGS

The name of this thick, creamy soup may be a bit of a tongue twister, but the texture of the soup is extra rich without the help of even one drop of cream. Celery root (or celeriac) is not particularly attractive—it's a gnarled bulb with a hairy-looking exterior—but once you peel away the skin, there's a gorgeous pale beige root with the unmistakable flavor of celery and a sweet earthiness. I wanted to add another dimension to the soup, so I fried capers in a little bit of olive oil. With their piquant, salty flavor, they make a great soup topping.

1 Tbsp olive oil
1 Tbsp butter
1 medium onion, chopped
Sea salt
Freshly ground black (or white) pepper

3 large celery roots or celeriac, peeled and chopped
6 cups [1.4 L] Vegetable Stock (page 34)
Fried Capers (page 166) for serving

1. In a large stockpot over low heat, warm the olive oil and butter until the butter is melted. Add the onion, season with salt and pepper, and cook, without allowing the onion to brown, for 5 minutes. Add the celery root and cook, stirring, for 2 minutes. Turn the heat to high, add the vegetable stock, and bring to a boil. Turn the heat to low, partially cover, and simmer for about 45 minutes, or until the celery root is very tender when tested with a small, sharp knife. Remove from the heat and let cool slightly.

2. Using a food processor or blender and working in batches or using a handheld immersion blender, purée the soup until smooth. Return the soup to the pot. Taste and adjust the seasoning, adding more salt and pepper if needed.

3. Ladle the soup into mugs or bowls and serve hot, topped with the fried capers.

> *TO GO: Fry the capers at home, let them cool, and pack them separately. The heat of the soup will warm them.*

All About Puréed Soups

- Buy yourself a handheld immersion blender. Like a long stick with a motorized blender unit at the end, immersion blenders let you purée soups directly in the pot without having to transfer the soup to a food processor or blender and then back to the stockpot. One pot gets dirty, and that's it. Best of all? With just a bit of comparison shopping, you should be able to find a perfectly serviceable two-speed immersion blender for a modest price.

- Always let your soup cool down for about 15 minutes before transferring it to a food processor or blender to purée. Very hot soup can "explode" and can be dangerous.

- When puréeing soups, always remember to fill the container of the food processor or blender a little under half full. Work in batches. An overfilled blender or food processor results in a huge mess.

- Purée your soup using equal parts stock and vegetables. In other words, don't purée all the thick stuff (vegetables) and then be left with a pot of thin liquid stock. You want to add equal amounts of stock and vegetables, working bit by bit, so you can gauge if the soup is too thick or thin.

- Always place a tea towel on top of the food processor or blender before blending to protect yourself and your kitchen in case the soup does "explode."

- If your soup is too thick, add more liquid/stock or even water. If it's too thin, simmer the soup, uncovered, for about 10 minutes, or until it reduces and thickens slightly.

CALIFORNIA CREAM OF ARTICHOKE SOUP

C V

MAKES 8 TASTING PORTIONS OR 4 TO 6 FULL PORTIONS

Here's the deal: You *can* make this soup with frozen artichoke hearts, but I think they tend to taste of citric acid. Instead, look for artichoke hearts that are steamed and vacuum sealed from Melissa's Produce. Better yet, look for fresh artichokes during spring, when they are in season and often on sale. If using frozen, thaw them before using and add a squeeze of fresh lemon juice before adding them to the soup. If using canned or jarred hearts, rinse them under cold running water and dry them thoroughly.

Serve with Croutes or Gremolata, both of which add great texture and flavor to this creamy soup. This is a very rich soup; a little goes a long way. Serve it with Citrus Salad with Crème Fraîche and Tarragon (page 159) as a light counterpoint.

6 fresh large artichokes or
  24 jarred, canned, steamed,
  or frozen artichoke quarters
1 large leek
1½ Tbsp olive oil
2 medium shallots, chopped
Sea salt

Freshly ground black pepper
½ cup [120 ml] dry white wine
3 cups [720 ml] Vegetable Stock
  (page 34)
2 Tbsp to ¼ cup [60 ml] heavy cream
1 tsp fresh lemon juice (optional)
Croutes (page 167) or Gremolata
  (page 165) for serving (optional)

1. If using fresh artichokes, trim off the stem end of the artichokes and put them in a large stockpot. Add enough boiling water to cover them and cook, covered, over medium-high heat for 16 to 18 minutes, or until a leaf can be pulled out easily. Drain and set aside to cool. Remove all the leaves from each artichoke (melt some butter, cut a lemon, and eat now while warm) and scoop out all the fuzz surrounding the heart. Chop the hearts and reserve.

2. Trim off the dark green section from the leek and save for making vegetable stock. Halve the pale green and white section lengthwise. Rinse under cold running water, pat dry, and cut cross-wise into thin pieces.

3. In a medium stockpot over low heat, warm the olive oil. Add the leek and shallots and cook, stirring, for 10 minutes. Add the artichoke hearts, season with salt and pepper, and cook, stirring, for another 3 minutes. Turn the heat to high, add the wine, and simmer for 2 minutes. Add the vegetable stock and bring to a boil. Turn the heat to low, cover, and simmer gently for 20 minutes, or until the artichokes are tender. Let cool slightly.

4. Using a food processor or blender and working in batches or using a handheld immersion blender, purée the soup until smooth. Return the soup to the pot, season with salt and pepper, and return the pot to low heat. Add the cream and lemon juice, if needed, and simmer for about 5 minutes.

5. Ladle the soup into mugs or bowls and serve topped with the croutes and/or gremolata, if desired.

TO GO: Pack the croutes and/or gremolata separately.

TOMATO SOUP
WITH GRILLED-CHEESE CROUTONS

C V

MAKES 8 TO 10 TASTING PORTIONS OR 6 FULL SERVINGS

The ultimate comfort meal—tomato soup with grilled cheese (croutons) on top. Obviously it is best to make this soup in the summer and fall, when fresh garden tomatoes are available, but there are some "acceptable" winter-tomato substitutes such as good-quality organic canned tomatoes or hothouse-grown organic winter tomatoes. Add ½ tsp sugar with the tomatoes if you are preparing this soup in winter. The Grilled-Cheese Croutons will appeal to kids as well as grown-ups.

2 medium leeks

1½ Tbsp olive oil

2 medium onions, thinly sliced

1 large shallot, chopped

2 lb [910 g] vine-ripened tomatoes

Sea salt

Freshly ground black pepper

4 cups [960 ml] Vegetable Stock (page 34)

¼ cup [60 ml] heavy cream (optional)

Grilled-Cheese Croutons (page 170), halved, for garnish

⅓ cup [20 g] fresh basil, cut into very fine ribbons

1. Trim off the dark green sections from the leeks and save for making vegetable stock. Halve the pale green and white sections lengthwise. Rinse under cold running water, pat dry, and cut crosswise into thin pieces.

2. In a large stockpot over low heat, warm the olive oil. Add the leeks, onions, and shallot and cook, stirring, for 10 minutes.

3. Meanwhile, bring a pot of water to a boil over high heat. Cut a small X in the stem end of each tomato. Drop the tomatoes into the boiling water and blanch them for about 20 seconds. Using a slotted spoon, transfer them to a colander to drain. When cool enough to handle, remove and discard the skin from the tomatoes, remove the core, and coarsely chop the flesh.

4. Add the tomatoes to the stockpot, season with salt and pepper, and cook for 5 minutes. Turn the heat to high, add the vegetable stock, and bring to a boil. Turn the heat to low and simmer for 30 minutes. Remove from the heat and let cool slightly.

5. Using a food processor or blender and working in batches or using a handheld immersion blender, purée the soup until smooth. Return the soup to the pot, add the cream (if using), and simmer over low heat for about 10 minutes. If the soup is too thin or watery, simmer for about another 10 minutes, until slightly thickened. Taste and adjust the seasoning, adding more salt and pepper if needed.

6. Ladle the soup into mugs or bowls and top each with 2 to 4 croutons or a half-slice of open-faced crouton, if you prefer. Garnish with the basil and serve.

TO GO: Prepare the croutons but instead of adding the basil and cheese and broiling them, place them on a baking sheet and cover with plastic wrap. Pack the basil and cheese separately. At the party, broil the croutons with the cheese and sprinkle with the basil just before serving with the soup.

Toast That Nut

Toasting nuts in a 350°F [180°C] oven is an easy way to make nuts taste . . . *nuttier.* Chopped toasted nuts add great flavor and texture to soups. This works with any type of nut: hazelnuts, almonds, walnuts, pistachio, Brazil nuts, pecans, and more.

Position a rack in the middle of the oven and preheat to 350°F [180°C]. Spread the nuts of your choice in a single layer on a rimmed baking sheet and toast them for 6 to 8 minutes, or until they are fragrant. The idea is not to brown the nuts (though many nuts will take on a richer, golden color) but to release their oils. Use your nose to tell you when the nuts are ready. Or taste one nut; it should taste nutty and richer than a raw one. Let cool. Store in a tightly sealed container for up to 1 week.

If you're toasting hazelnuts with skins on, remove the baking sheet from the oven after 10 minutes and transfer the nuts to one half of a clean tea towel. Fold the free half of the tea towel over the nuts, and rub them back and forth with the towel to remove their skin before chopping.

BABY TURNIP SOUP
WITH MISO BUTTER AND TOASTED HAZELNUTS

MAKES 10 TO 12 TASTING PORTIONS OR 8 FULL SERVINGS

Laced with cream, dusted with toasted chopped hazelnuts, and finished with a swirl of simple miso-flavored butter, this light soup delivers plenty of texture and flavor.

Look for baby white Japanese turnips or farm-grown small red turnips at farmers' markets and specialty stores. Try to avoid using those huge grapefruit-size turnips (frequently coated in wax), as they are quite starchy and not at all light and juicy like the smaller farm-fresh vegetables. Turnips are available from late spring throughout the winter and, like so many other root vegetables, can withstand a good deal of cold temperatures.

Serve the soup with Mixed Greens Salad with Mint-Tangerine Vinaigrette (page 156).

2 medium-large leeks or 1 large Vidalia onion, thinly sliced
2½ Tbsp olive oil
1½ lb [680 g] baby white or red turnips, trimmed, and cut into ½-in [12-mm] pieces
Sea salt
Freshly ground black pepper
8 cups [2 L] Vegetable Stock (page 34)
¼ to ⅓ cup [60 to 80 ml] heavy cream
1 cup [110 g] hazelnuts, toasted (see facing page) and coarsely chopped
Miso Butter (page 164) for serving

1. Trim off the dark green sections from the leeks and save for making vegetable stock. Halve the pale green and white sections lengthwise. Rinse under cold running water, pat dry, and cut crosswise into thin pieces.

2. In a medium stockpot over low heat, warm the olive oil. Add the leeks and stir to coat with the oil. Cover and cook for 8 minutes. Add the turnips, season with salt and pepper, and stir. Cover and cook for another 8 minutes. Turn the heat to high, add the vegetable stock, and bring to a boil. Turn the heat to medium-low and simmer, partially covered, for about 20 minutes, or until the turnips are tender and the broth is flavorful. Remove from the heat and let cool for 5 minutes.

3. Using a food processor or blender and working in batches or using a handheld immersion blender, purée the soup until smooth. Return the soup to the pot and bring to a simmer over medium heat; simmer vigorously for 5 to 8 minutes, until reduced and thickened. Turn the heat to low. When the soup is simmering gently, stir in the cream. Taste and adjust the seasoning, adding more salt and pepper if needed. Simmer for another 2 to 3 minutes.

4. Ladle the soup into mugs or bowls and serve with the toasted hazelnuts and the miso butter.

TO GO: Pack the toasted hazelnuts and miso butter separately. Bring a pot to the party to reheat the butter. (If all the burners are in use, reheat in a 300°F [180°C] oven until warm.) Add the miso butter and nuts just before serving.

ROASTED FALL-VEGETABLE SOUP

MAKES 10 TO 12 TASTING PORTIONS OR 6 TO 8 FULL SERVINGS

When you roast winter root vegetables along with shallots, leeks, and garlic, they caramelize and become sweet. Although this soup takes about an hour from start to finish, the resulting flavor is startlingly complex. It's important to cut the vegetables about the same size to ensure even cooking.

3 medium leeks

3 medium parsnips, peeled and cut crosswise into ½-in [12-mm] pieces

3 medium carrots, peeled and cut crosswise into ½-in [12-mm] pieces

One 2-lb [910-g] butternut squash or any type of winter squash, peeled and cut into ½-in [12-mm] cubes

2 large or 3 medium celery stalks, cut crosswise into ½-in [12-mm] pieces

1 medium celery root, peeled and cut into ½-in [12-mm] cubes

2 shallots, quartered

8 garlic cloves, thinly sliced

1½ Tbsp chopped fresh thyme leaves, or 2 tsp dried

3 Tbsp olive oil

Sea salt

Freshly ground black pepper

5 cups [1.2 L] Vegetable Stock (page 34) or canned low-sodium broth

¾ cup [180 ml] dry white wine

Parsley Pesto (page 165) for serving

Double-Cheese Croutes (page 168) for serving

|||||||||||||||||||||||||||||||||

1. Position a rack in the middle of the oven and preheat to 400°F [200°C].

2. Trim off the dark green sections from the leeks and save for making vegetable stock. Halve the pale green and white sections lengthwise. Rinse under cold running water, pat dry, and cut crosswise into ½-in [12-mm] pieces.

3. In one large or two medium very shallow roasting pan(s) or rimmed baking sheet(s), combine the leeks, parsnips, carrots, squash, celery, celery root, shallots, garlic, and thyme. Drizzle with the olive oil, season with salt and pepper, and toss to evenly coat the vegetables. You don't want to have vegetables on top of one another; you want them in a single layer.

4. Roast the vegetables for 20 minutes. Turn the oven temperature to 450°F [230°C] and roast for another 10 minutes, or until the vegetables are a nice golden brown, almost crispy on the edges, and almost soft when you gently test them with a fork or small, sharp knife. You don't want them soft and mushy; they will continue cooking in the soup.

5. Meanwhile, in a large stockpot over high heat, bring the vegetable stock to a boil. Turn the heat to medium-low and gently simmer.

6. Remove the vegetables from the oven, add the wine, and deglaze the pan, using a spatula to loosen any bits clinging to the bottom. Pour everything from the baking sheet into the stock. Turn the heat to low and simmer, partially covered, for 20 to 30 minutes. Taste and adjust the seasoning, adding more salt and pepper if needed.

7. Ladle the soup into mugs or bowls and serve piping hot, topped with the pesto and croutes.

TO GO: Pack the pesto and croutes separately.

ROASTED CARROT AND GINGER SOUP

MAKES 10 TO 12 TASTING PORTIONS OR 8 FULL SERVINGS

Everyone's on a special diet these days; gluten-free, dairy-free, vegan, vegetarian. Guess what? This soup can be served to everyone. Ginger adds a fresh, crisp, biting nuance to this soup when it's roasted with carrots and leeks and then combined with a strongly steeped cup of ginger tea. If you want a multilayered ginger experience, top the finished soup with some peeled and grated fresh ginger or thin strips of crystalized ginger. Grate the fresh ginger with a Microplane or the fine holes of a cheese grater directly onto the soup. Thanks to cookbook author, writer, and friend Molly O'Neill for the brilliant ginger tea and freshly grated ginger ideas.

The puréed soup can be served as is or topped with a dollop of plain Greek yogurt or a swirl of heavy cream (apologies, vegans), chopped fresh chives, or Croutes (page 167; sorry, gluten-free friends) or Polenta Croutons (page 169).

4 small or 2 large leeks
10 medium carrots, peeled and cut crosswise into 2-in [5-cm] pieces
3 Tbsp olive oil
Sea salt
Freshly ground black pepper
One 2-in [5-cm] piece fresh ginger, peeled and coarsely chopped, plus freshly grated, peeled ginger for garnish (optional)
1 ginger tea bag
8 cups [2 L] Vegetable Stock (page 34)

1. Position a rack in the middle of the oven and preheat to 400°F [200°C].

2. Trim off the dark green sections from the leeks and save for making vegetable stock. Halve the pale green and white sections lengthwise. Rinse under cold running water, pat dry, and cut crosswise into ½-in [12-mm] pieces.

3. In a medium roasting pan or ovenproof skillet, combine the carrots and leeks. Drizzle with the olive oil, season with salt and pepper, and toss to evenly coat the vegetables.

4. Roast the vegetables for 15 minutes. Remove the pan from the oven and toss the vegetables. Stir in the chopped ginger and roast for another 15 minutes.

5. Meanwhile, in a kettle, bring 1 cup [240 ml] water to a boil. Make a cup of tea with the ginger tea bag and steep for 5 minutes. Remove the bag, squeezing it to release all the liquid.

6. In a large stockpot over high heat, warm the vegetable stock.

7. Remove the roasting pan from the oven and deglaze with the ginger tea, scraping up any bits clinging to the bottom of the pan. Pour all the vegetables and liquid into the stockpot. Bring to a boil. Turn the heat to low, cover, and simmer for 30 minutes. Remove the soup from the heat and let cool slightly.

8. Using a food processor or blender and working in batches or using a handheld immersion blender, purée the soup until smooth. Return the soup to the pot. Taste and adjust the seasoning, adding more salt and pepper if needed.

9. Ladle the soup into mugs or bowls and serve topped with freshly grated ginger, if desired.

TO GO: If you're adding grated ginger to the finished soup, grate it at home and pack it separately or bring peeled ginger and a Microplane grater to the party and let guests grate the ginger for themselves.

ROASTED PUMPKIN SOUP
WITH FRIED SAGE LEAVES

MAKES 10 TO 12 TASTING PORTIONS OR 8 FULL SERVINGS

To make this gorgeous, pale orange soup, look for small sugar pumpkins (such as Baby Bear, Wee-B-Little, Cinderella, or Long Island Cheese, to name just a few) as opposed to Halloween carving pumpkins. Serve with Skillet Corn Bread with Chive and Brown Butter (page 154).

One 3-lb [1.4-kg] sugar pumpkin or winter squash

2 medium leeks

1 Tbsp chopped fresh thyme

1 Tbsp chopped fresh sage

Sea salt

Freshly ground black pepper

2 Tbsp olive oil

8 cups [2 L] Vegetable Stock (page 34)

1 cup [240 ml] heavy cream, crème fraîche, or plain Greek yogurt

16 leaves of Fried Sage (see page 166)

1. Position a rack in the middle of the oven and preheat to 425°F [220°C].

2. Using a wide peeler or sharp knife, remove the rind from the pumpkin. Cut the pumpkin in half and remove the seeds and the stringy sections. Cut the flesh into 1½-in [4-cm] cubes.

3. Trim off the dark green sections from the leeks and save for making vegetable stock. Halve the pale green and white sections lengthwise. Rinse under cold running water, pat dry, and cut crosswise into ½-in [12-mm] pieces.

4. On a large rimmed baking sheet or in a shallow baking dish or roasting pan, combine the pumpkin, leeks, ½ Tbsp of the thyme, and ½ Tbsp of the sage. Drizzle with the olive oil, season with salt and pepper, and toss to evenly coat the vegetables.

5. Roast the vegetables for about 20 minutes, or until they begin to turn golden brown. If the vegetables appear to be burning or getting too dark, turn the oven temperature to 375°F [190°C] and cover them loosely with aluminum foil.

6. Meanwhile, in a large stockpot over high heat, bring the vegetable stock to a boil. Add the remaining ½ Tbsp thyme and ½ Tbsp sage and turn the heat to low.

7. Remove the vegetables from the oven. Pour everything from the baking sheet into the stock. Be sure to scrape up any bits clinging to the bottom of the baking sheet. Cover and simmer for about 15 minutes, or until the pumpkin is tender when tested with a small, sharp knife. Remove from the heat and let cool slightly.

8. Using a food processor or blender and working in batches or using a handheld immersion blender, purée the soup until smooth. Return the soup to the pot. Taste and adjust the seasoning, adding more salt and pepper if needed.

9. Ladle the soup into mugs or bowls and top each with 1 tsp of the cream (don't stir; just swirl it in). Add a fried sage leaf and serve.

TO GO: Make the Fried Sage about 1 hour ahead and pack loosely in paper towels.

CHESTNUT SOUP
WITH MUSHROOM-THYME SAUTÉ

GF V

MAKES 12 TO 14 TASTING PORTIONS OR 10 FULL SERVINGS

I was never particularly intrigued by the idea of chestnut soup. But on a recent trip to northern Italy, I was served a rich purée of chestnuts and was instantly converted.

Rich, silky, and ideal for the holidays, this soup should be served in small bowls (or even shot glasses). Top with a spoonful of Mushroom-Thyme Sauté or a dollop of crème fraîche or sour cream, or just sprinkle with minced fresh chives and fresh thyme or with microgreens. You can find good-quality roasted chestnuts in glass jars or plastic pouches. Look for them in specialty food shops. Serve with Citrus Salad with Crème Fraîche and Tarragon (page 159).

2 large leeks
2 Tbsp olive oil or butter
3 Tbsp chopped fresh thyme
15 oz [430 g] whole roasted chestnuts, chopped
Sea salt
Freshly ground black pepper

½ cup [120 ml] cream sherry or dry sherry
8 cups [2 L] Vegetable Stock (page 34)
⅔ cup [160 ml] heavy cream

GARNISHES
3 Tbsp finely chopped fresh thyme and chives
Mushroom-Thyme Sauté (page 171)
Dollop of crème fraîche or sour cream

1. Trim off the dark green sections from the leeks and save for making vegetable stock. Halve the pale green and white sections lengthwise. Rinse under cold running water, pat dry, and cut crosswise into thin pieces.

2. In a large stockpot over low heat, warm the olive oil. Add the leeks, cover, and cook, stirring once or twice, for 8 minutes. Remove the lid, stir in the thyme and chestnuts, and season with salt and pepper. Cook, stirring, for 1 minute. Turn the heat to high, add the sherry, and cook for 2 minutes. Add the vegetable stock and bring to a boil. Turn the heat to low, partially cover, and cook for 15 minutes. Remove from the heat and add the cream. Let cool slightly.

3. Using a food processor or blender and working in batches or using a handheld immersion blender, purée the soup until smooth. Return the soup to the pot, turn the heat to medium, and bring to a simmer. If the soup is too thin, simmer for another 10 to 15 minutes until slightly thickened. Taste and adjust the seasoning, adding more salt and pepper if needed.

4. Ladle the soup into mugs or bowls and serve piping hot with any or all of the garnishes.

TO GO: Pack the garnishes separately. The Mushroom-Thyme Sauté can be reheated over a free burner or in a 300°F [150°C] oven for 10 to 12 minutes, or until hot.

FIVE-MUSHROOM SOUP
WITH MUSHROOM-THYME SAUTÉ

GF V

MAKES 10 TO 12 TASTING PORTIONS OR 8 FULL SERVINGS

There are two secrets to this soup: First, roasted mushrooms add an almost smoky, earthy flavor dimension. Second, the soup calls for five types of mushrooms. The more varieties you use, the more dimension you add to the soup, but feel free to prepare it with just one or two varieties if that's all you have on hand.

The soup is ready when your kitchen smells like you've taken a walk deep into the forest. A thick, chunky blend, it has a naturally creamy consistency, but if you want to indulge, add just ¼ cup [60 ml] or less of heavy cream, crème fraîche, or Greek yogurt. Mushroom-Thyme Sauté is the ideal topping for this soup. Serve with Buttery Biscuits (page 155).

1 lb [455 g] portobello mushrooms, ends trimmed and caps quartered

8 oz [230 g] shiitake mushrooms, cleaned, ends trimmed, and caps halved

8 oz [230 g] cremini mushrooms, cleaned, ends trimmed, and caps halved

8 oz [230 g] maitake (also called hen of the woods), cleaned, ends trimmed, and then quartered

1 medium onion, chopped

2 medium shallots, chopped

1½ Tbsp chopped fresh thyme

2 Tbsp olive oil

Sea salt

Freshly ground black pepper

½ cup [230 g] dried porcini or dried mushrooms of your choice

8 cups [2 L] Vegetable Stock (page 34)

3 Tbsp dry red wine or dry sherry

¼ cup [60 ml] heavy cream or plain Greek yogurt (optional)

Mushroom-Thyme Sauté (page 171) for serving

1. Position a rack in the middle of the oven and preheat to 400°F [200°C].

2. In a large roasting pan, combine the portobello, shiitake, cremini, and maitake mushrooms with the onion, shallots, and ½ Tbsp of the thyme. Drizzle with the olive oil, season with salt and pepper, and toss to evenly coat the vegetables.

3. Roast the vegetables for 15 minutes. Remove the pan from the oven, toss the mixture, and roast for another 15 minutes. The mushrooms should be soft (but still holding their shape) and the onion should be beginning to turn golden brown. The mushrooms will shrink and lose their water; do not be concerned if the roasting pan looks like it contains half the number of mushrooms you started with.

4. Meanwhile, in a small bowl, soak the dried mushrooms in 1 cup [240 ml] hot water for 10 minutes. Drain the mushrooms, pat dry, and chop. Strain the soaking liquid and set aside.

continued

5. In a large stockpot over medium-high heat, bring the vegetable stock and ½ Tbsp thyme to a simmer.

6. Remove the roasting pan from the oven and deglaze with the wine, scraping up any bits clinging to the bottom of the pan. Pour all the vegetables and liquid into the simmering stock. Add the dried mushrooms and the soaking liquid and simmer, covered, for 30 to 45 minutes. The soup should have a distinct mushroom flavor. Taste and adjust the seasoning, adding more salt and pepper if needed.

7. Using a food processor or blender and working in batches or using a handheld immersion blender, purée the soup, leaving it a bit chunky. Return the soup to the pot and bring to a gentle simmer over low heat. Taste and adjust the seasoning, adding more salt and pepper if needed, and add the cream if desired.

8. Ladle the soup into mugs or bowls and serve topped with the remaining thyme and some of the mushroom sauté.

TO GO: Pack the thyme and the Mushroom-Thyme Sauté separately and bring a small ovenproof skillet to heat it just before serving the soup. If all the burners are in use, you can reheat it in a 300°F [150°C] oven.

FRENCH ONION SOUP
WITH DOUBLE-CHEESE CROUTES

MAKES 10 TO 12 TASTING PORTIONS OR 8 FULL SERVINGS

This classic French soup is made with rich beef stock and a heavy blanket of sautéed onions and leeks. You can lighten it up a bit by serving the soup as is, without the traditional cheese and bread topping. In Parisian bistros, onion soup is prepared in an ovenproof bowl, topped with a slice of crusty bread, smothered with grated Gruyère, and then broiled. I find this method a bit heavy-handed. I like to serve the soup topped with a double-cheese croute, which calls to mind the comforting bread and cheese topping that is so much a part of the classic recipe without masking the natural richness of the soup.

If there's any way you can make this soup a day ahead, you should do so. The onions, stock, and wine all "settle down" overnight and become good friends. This is a main-course soup where homemade beef stock really pays off. Serve with red wine and Mixed Greens Salad with Mint-Tangerine Vinaigrette (page 156).

3 large leeks

2½ Tbsp olive oil

1½ Tbsp butter

3 lb [1.4 kg] onions, yellow and red or just yellow, very thinly sliced

Sea salt

Freshly ground black pepper

1¼ cups [300 ml] dry red wine

¼ cup [60 ml] Cognac

7 cups [1.7 L] Basic Beef Stock (page 27), Rich Beef-Bone Broth (page 24), or canned low-sodium broth

8 to 12 Double-Cheese Croutes (page 168)

½ cup [30 g] packed chopped fresh parsley

||||||||||||||||||||||||||||||||||

1. Trim off the dark green sections from the leeks and save for making vegetable stock. Halve the pale green and white sections lengthwise. Rinse under cold running water, pat dry, and cut crosswise into thin pieces.

2. In a large skillet, or two medium skillets, over very low heat, warm the olive oil and butter. Add the leeks and onions to the skillet(s) and cook, stirring occasionally, for about 1 hour, or until the onions are buttery and soft but not brown. Season with salt and pepper. Turn the heat to medium-high, add the wine and Cognac, and bring to a boil. Continue to boil for 3 minutes.

3. In a large stockpot over high heat, bring the beef stock to a boil. Add the onions, leeks, and all the liquid to the stock, scraping up any bits clinging to the bottom of the skillet(s). Turn the heat to low, partially cover, and simmer for about 1 hour. Taste the soup. It should be very flavorful. If the flavor is weak, turn the heat to medium-high and simmer vigorously for another 10 minutes.

4. Ladle the soup into mugs or bowls, top each with a croute, and sprinkle with fresh parsley. Serve immediately.

TO GO: Pack the croutes and parsley in separate containers.

ESCAROLE AND WHITE BEAN SOUP
WITH PARMESAN CHEESE

MAKES 10 TO 12 TASTING PORTIONS OR 8 FULL SERVINGS

Escarole, a slightly bitter variety of endive, looks like a big head of lettuce with broad leaves and a wonderful crunch. High in folic acid and fiber, it's loaded with vitamins and makes an excellent soup. This is a thick, warming soup with white cannellini beans and lots of garlic. If you have a Parmesan cheese rind in your freezer, add it to the soup; before serving, be sure to remove it with a slotted spoon. The soup has a surprisingly complex flavor but takes well under an hour to make! You could also top the soup with some cooked, crumbled pancetta or bacon. Serve with Mixed Greens Salad with Mint-Tangerine Vinaigrette (page 156).

2 lb [910 g] escarole

2 medium leeks or 2 medium sweet onions

1½ Tbsp olive oil

4 garlic cloves, thinly sliced

2½ tsp chopped fresh thyme

Sea salt

Freshly ground black pepper

3 cups [660 g] cooked white cannellini beans (see page 107), or canned beans (drained, rinsed, and re-drained)

7 cups [1.7 L] Vegetable Stock (page 34)

Parmesan cheese rind (optional), plus ½ cup [40 g] freshly grated Parmesan cheese

1. Core the escarole. Rinse under cold water and thoroughly dry. Finely chop one half and coarsely chop the other half; set aside. Trim off the dark green sections from the leeks and save for making vegetable stock. Halve the pale green and white sections lengthwise. Rinse under cold running water, pat dry, and cut crosswise into thin pieces. (If using onions, cut them into thin slices.)

2. In a large stockpot over low heat, warm the olive oil. Add the leeks and garlic and cook, stirring, for 5 minutes. Add 1¼ tsp of the thyme and season with salt and pepper.

3. Using a food processor or blender, purée 1 cup [220 g] of the beans, the remaining 1¼ tsp thyme, and 1 cup [240 ml] of the vegetable stock until smooth. Add the bean purée and remaining 2 cups [440 g] beans to the pot. Turn the heat to medium, add all the escarole, and cook, stirring, for 4 to 5 minutes, or until the leaves are just wilted. Turn the heat to high, add the remaining 6 cups [1.4 L] vegetable stock, and bring to a boil. Add the Parmesan rind (if using), turn the heat to low, and cook, partially covered, for 15 minutes. Taste and adjust the seasoning, adding more salt and pepper if needed. Remove the rind from the soup.

4. Ladle the soup into bowls and serve hot, sprinkled with grated cheese.

TO GO: *Pack the grated cheese separately.*

MINESTRONE SOUP

MAKES 10 TO 12 TASTING PORTIONS OR 8 FULL SERVINGS

There are endless variations of this Italian classic. You can use any, or all, of the vegetables listed here. I also like to add a small amount of leftover baked or boiled potato and a tiny soup pasta called *acini di pepe*. If you've saved a Parmesan cheese rind (see page 77 for more on freezing rinds), by all means add it to the soup along with the tomatoes—but don't forget to remove it with a slotted spoon before serving.

Be sure to top the soup with chopped fresh parsley and freshly grated Parmesan cheese. This is a very hearty, filling soup—ideal for a cold winter's night. Serve with warm crusty bread.

2 medium leeks

1½ Tbsp olive oil

2 garlic cloves, chopped

2 medium carrots, peeled and cut crosswise into ½-in [12-mm] pieces

1 medium parsnip, peeled and cut crosswise into ½-in [12-mm] pieces

2 large celery stalks, cut crosswise into ½-in [12-mm] pieces

1 medium zucchini, ends trimmed and chopped into ½-in [12-mm] pieces

1 Tbsp finely chopped fresh rosemary

½ cup [30 g] packed finely chopped fresh parsley

Sea salt

Freshly ground black pepper

1½ tsp tomato paste

2 medium ripe tomatoes, cored and cut into ½-in [12-mm] pieces, or 2 cups [440 g] good-quality canned crushed Italian tomatoes

1 Parmesan cheese rind (optional), plus 1 cup [80 g] freshly grated Parmesan cheese

2 cups [440 g] cooked white cannellini beans (see page 107), or canned beans (drained, rinsed, and re-drained)

8 oz [230 g] cooked Yukon gold or russet potatoes, peeled and cut into ½-in [12-mm] pieces (optional)

6 cups [1.4 L] Vegetable Stock (page 34)

Pinch of red chili flakes

¼ cup [30 g] *acini di pepe* or very small soup pasta

Parmesan Cheese Crisps (page 168) for serving (optional)

Parsley Pesto (page 165) for serving (optional)

1. Trim off the dark green sections from the leeks and save for making vegetable stock. Halve the pale green and white sections lengthwise. Rinse under cold running water, pat dry, and cut crosswise into ½-in [12-mm] pieces.

2. In a large stockpot over low heat, warm the olive oil. Add the garlic and cook for 1 minute. Add the leeks, cover, and cook, stirring once or twice, for 6 minutes. Add the carrots, parsnip, celery, zucchini, rosemary, and half of the parsley and season with salt and pepper. Turn the heat to medium and cook, stirring, for 5 minutes. The vegetables should be just beginning to turn gold. Add the tomato paste, stir to coat the vegetables, and cook another 2 minutes. Add the tomatoes, Parmesan rind (if using), beans, and potatoes (if using) and stir well. Turn the heat to high, add the vegetable stock, and bring to a boil. Turn the heat to low, add the red chili flakes, and simmer, partially covered, for 15 minutes. Taste and adjust the seasoning, adding more salt and pepper if needed. If the soup is not as flavorful as you like, remove the lid and simmer it over medium heat for another 10 minutes.

continued

3. Add the pasta to the soup and simmer for 10 minutes more, or until the pasta is al dente, or just barely tender. (Remember you will be reheating the soup, so you want to slightly under-cook the pasta. Cooking the pasta directly in the soup will work only if you're using a very small shape. If using orzo or a larger shape, boil separately for about 7 minutes, drain, and then add to the soup. See page 97 for more about cooking pasta.) Remove the rind from the soup.

4. Ladle the soup into mugs or bowls. Top with the remaining parsley and some grated cheese before serving. Pass the cheese crisps and pesto separately, if desired.

TO GO: Pack the grated cheese and the parsley separately. If serving the pesto and the Parmesan Cheese Crisps, pack them separately as well.

Why Is There a Cheese Rind in My Soup?

Real Parmesan cheese (Parmigiano-Reggiano) is so full of flavor that when I'm done grating it into soup, over salads, or on top of pasta, I always save the rind. Yes, the rind is also packed with flavor.

I cut the rind into three small pieces, place them in a tightly sealed plastic bag, and freeze them for up to three months. Then, when I'm making an Italian soup or any soup where Parmesan cheese is one of the ingredients, I pull out the frozen rind and add a piece to my soup. It infuses the soup with a meatiness and depth of flavor that is extraordinary. Be sure to remove the rind with a slotted spoon before serving.

MULLIGATAWNY SOUP

MAKES 10 TO 12 TASTING PORTIONS OR 8 FULL SERVINGS

Layers of taste—that's how I'd describe this soup. There's sweet coconut milk, ginger, and garlic, and then another layer of soft red lentils and pungent Indian spices. Just before serving, each bowl of soup is topped with a spicy and savory hot butter sauce spiked with chile, scallion, and chopped tomato. You can control the amount of heat by adding more or less of the chile in the soup and the topping.

This recipe is an adaptation of one from legendary cookbook author, Indian food expert, and actress Madhur Jaffrey.

TOMATO-CHILE TOPPING

3 Tbsp lightly salted butter
¾ tsp black mustard seeds
¾ tsp cumin seeds
⅛ tsp ground cumin
⅛ tsp garam masala
1 dried red chile pepper, crumbled
2 Tbsp finely chopped scallion
1 small ripe tomato, finely chopped
Sea salt
Freshly ground black pepper

SOUP

1 Tbsp canola oil
1 Tbsp butter
3 garlic cloves, finely chopped
One 2-in [5-cm] piece fresh ginger, peeled and finely chopped
2 scallions, chopped
¼ to ½ Tbsp finely chopped fresh jalapeño chile, with or without seeds (wear kitchen gloves and be careful not to get the seeds anywhere near your eyes)
Sea salt
Freshly ground black pepper
1 tsp ground cumin
1 tsp garam masala
2 Tbsp all-purpose flour
2 Tbsp finely chopped fresh cilantro, plus ½ cup [20 g]
1½ cups [330 g] split red lentils
8 cups [2 L] Basic Chicken Stock (page 29)
1 cup [240 ml] canned whole coconut milk, preferably organic
2 to 3 Tbsp fresh lemon juice
1 cup [240 ml] plain Greek yogurt or whole-fat yogurt

1. **TO MAKE THE TOPPING:** In a small skillet over low heat, warm the butter. Add the mustard seeds, cumin seeds, ground cumin, garam masala, and dried chile pepper and cook for 2 minutes. Add the scallion and tomato, season with salt and pepper, and cook for another 3 minutes, or until the mixture is bubbling and fragrant. Remove from the heat. (The topping can be made several hours ahead. When cool, store in a small covered glass jar.)

2. **TO MAKE THE SOUP:** In a large stockpot over low heat, warm the canola oil and butter. When the butter is bubbling, add the garlic, ginger, and half of the scallions and cook, stirring, for 5 minutes. Add the jalapeño, season with salt and pepper, and cook for 2 minutes. Add the cumin and garam masala and cook, stirring, for 1 minute more. Sprinkle the flour over the mixture and stir it into the spices until blended; cook for 2 minutes. Stir in the 2 Tbsp cilantro and turn the heat to medium-high. Stir in the lentils and cook for 30 seconds. Add the chicken stock and bring to a boil. Turn the heat to low, cover, and simmer for 25 to

30 minutes, or until the lentils are soft and tender. Remove from the heat.

3. Using a food processor or blender and working in batches or using a handheld immersion blender, purée the soup until smooth. Return the soup to the pot. Taste and adjust the seasoning, adding more salt and pepper if needed. Add the coconut milk, lemon juice, and ¼ cup [10 g] cilantro and simmer over low heat for 5 minutes.

4. Ladle the soup into mugs or bowls. Drizzle each with a tiny bit of the hot topping (it can be quite spicy), sprinkle with the remaining cilantro and scallion, top with a dollop of yogurt, and serve.

TO GO: Pack the topping, cilantro, scallion, and yogurt in separate containers and bring a small oven-proof skillet. When you arrive at the party, reheat the topping over low heat (or if all the burners are in use, reheat it in a 300°F [150°C] oven until just sizzling) and let the guests add as much or as little as they like.

CORN AND SWEET-POTATO CHOWDER
WITH SAFFRON CREAM

MAKE 8 TO 10 TASTING PORTIONS OR 6 FULL SERVINGS

Fresh corn and sweet potatoes make a good team. The broth in this chowder is a gorgeous sunflower yellow, thanks to the saffron, sweet potatoes, and corn. It's best to make this chowder during corn season (late summer/early fall), so you'll have fresh, sweet corn and can use the husks to help flavor the broth. Serve with Buttery Biscuits (page 155) or Skillet Corn Bread with Chive and Brown Butter (page 154).

6 large ears fresh corn or 5 cups [700 g] frozen corn kernels

2 Tbsp olive oil

1 large onion, finely chopped

1 large yellow bell pepper, seeded, deribbed, and cut into ½-in [12-mm] squares

1 small red bell pepper, cut into ½-in [12-mm] squares

1 large sweet potato, peeled and cut into ½-in [12-mm] squares

Sea salt

Freshly ground black pepper

1 Tbsp all-purpose flour

4 cups [960 ml] Vegetable Stock (page 34)

¾ cup [180 ml] heavy cream

1 tsp crumbled saffron threads

2 scallions, trimmed, white and green sections very thinly sliced

1 Tbsp minced fresh chives

1. If using fresh corn, shuck the ears, remove the silks, and trim off the end so that you can stand the cob flat. Using a sharp knife and standing each cob on its end inside a large bowl, remove the kernels from the cob by working the knife straight down against the cob. Using the blunt side of the knife, scrape down the cob after the kernels have been removed to release the corn "milk." Mix the milk and corn kernels and set aside. Do not throw out the cobs.

2. In a large stockpot over medium-low heat, warm the olive oil. Add the onion and cook, stirring occasionally, for 8 minutes, or until translucent. Add half of the yellow bell pepper and half of the red bell pepper and cook for 3 minutes. Add the sweet potato, season with salt and pepper, and cook for 5 minutes. Stir in the flour and cook, stirring well to coat all the vegetables, for 2 minutes. Turn the heat to high, gently whisk in the vegetable stock,

and bring to a boil. Add the corncobs (not the corn kernels). Turn the heat to low, cover, and cook for 5 to 8 minutes, or until the potato is almost tender.

3. In a small saucepan over low heat, warm the cream and saffron and steep for 5 minutes.

4. Add the saffron cream, corn kernels, and corn "milk" to the stockpot and simmer for 5 minutes. Taste and adjust the seasoning, adding more salt and pepper if needed. Using tongs, remove the cobs from the pot and, holding each one over the pot, use a knife to scrape off any bits of chowder or corn clinging to the cob.

5. Ladle the chowder into mugs or bowls; sprinkle with the scallions, chives, and remaining red and yellow bell peppers; and serve.

TO GO: Pack the scallions, chives, and additional bell pepper separately and serve them at the party in small bowls.

CHICKEN & TURKEY SOUPS

What could possibly be more soothing than a bowl of chicken soup? There have been many scientific studies attempting to explain how chicken soup makes sick people feel healthier. I think the answer lies beyond science. I think a bowl of chicken soup is a symbol of love, home, and comfort. I believe it's really that simple.

But chicken soup is only the beginning. This collection of chicken- and turkey-based soups has traveled from Greece, Italy, Mexico, and Thailand. It seems the world knows no bounds when it comes to the love and healing powers of chicken soup.

YIA YIA'S GREEK AVGOLEMONO

(DF)

MAKES 12 TO 14 TASTING PORTIONS OR 8 TO 10 FULL SERVINGS

My friends John and Jane Angelopoulos were bragging about the version of this classic Greek chicken-lemon-orzo soup that John's mother, Theodora, makes. They told me how different it is from traditional *avgolemono* because the eggs are whipped in a blender until frothy and then whisked into hot chicken stock. John and Jane were kind enough to invite me into their kitchen for a lesson. (Spoiler alert: This soup is amazing!)

This is comfort food in the extreme, like a thick, lemony, chicken-filled porridge. You can make it as thick or as thin as you like, depending on the amount of chicken stock you add. If you have cooked chicken and chicken stock ready to go, this soup can be made in less than 30 minutes.

11 to 12 cups [2.6 to 2.8 L] Basic Chicken Stock (page 29), Roasted Chicken Stock (page 30), or canned low-sodium broth

1½ cups [250 g] orzo

4 cups [430 g] shredded or chopped cooked chicken

1 cup [240 ml] fresh lemon juice

Sea salt

Freshly ground black pepper

6 eggs, separated

2 Tbsp cornstarch

½ cup [20 g] chopped fresh parsley

1. In a large stockpot over medium heat, bring 11 cups [2.6 L] of the chicken stock to a simmer. Add the orzo and cook for about 8 minutes, or until the pasta is almost tender. Remove from the heat, add the chicken and lemon juice, and season with salt and pepper.

2. Meanwhile, using a blender on high speed, whip the egg whites for 1 to 2 minutes, until they are frothy and very white. Add the egg yolks, one at a time, blending after each addition. Add the cornstarch and blend until frothy and the cornstarch is fully incorporated. Remove the container from the blender and whisk in 1 cup [240 ml] of the hot chicken stock.

3. Whisk the egg mixture into the soup until it is smooth. If the soup begins to separate, simply whisk it vigorously. Turn the heat to low and simmer gently for 5 to 10 minutes, or until the soup is hot and the mixture is thickened. Taste and adjust the seasoning, adding more salt and pepper if needed. If the soup is too thick, add ½ to 1 cup [120 to 240 ml] of the remaining stock and heat through.

4. Ladle the soup into mugs or bowls and serve sprinkled with the parsley.

TO GO: Remove the pot from the heat before adding the egg mixture to the soup and whisk off the heat until smooth. Reheat at the party and adjust the seasoning as needed. Pack the parsley separately and let all the guests add their own.

STRACCIATELLA

MAKES 10 TO 12 TASTING PORTIONS OR 6 TO 8 FULL SERVINGS

How can a soup with such basic ingredients be transformed into something so utterly satisfying? This is a classic Roman soup—chicken stock, spinach, eggs, and freshly grated Parmesan cheese. When the eggs and cheese are whisked into the hot stock, they look like "little rags," or "little shreds," the definition of the Italian word *stracciatella*.

Because there are so few ingredients, it is really important to use the best-quality chicken stock, garden-fresh spinach, fresh eggs, and authentic Parmigiano-Reggiano. Serve with Burnt Radicchio Salad with Herbed Ricotta and Nuts (page 157).

8 cups [2 L] Basic Chicken Stock (page 29), Roasted Chicken Stock (page 30), or canned low-sodium broth

Sea salt

Freshly ground black pepper

5 eggs

¾ cup [60 g] freshly grated Parmesan cheese

5 cups [300 g] packed baby spinach or regular spinach, stems removed, washed and thoroughly dried, and thinly sliced

||||||||||||||||||||||||||||||

1. In a medium-large stockpot over high heat, bring the chicken stock to a boil and season with just a touch of salt and a generous grinding of pepper.

2. In a medium bowl, whisk together the eggs and ½ cup [40 g] of the grated cheese and season with salt and pepper.

3. Turn the heat to medium and add the spinach to the pot. As soon as the spinach leaves begin to wilt, use a fork to gradually whisk in the egg-cheese mixture until it resembles shreds. Turn the heat to low and cook for about 2 minutes. Taste and adjust the seasoning, adding more salt and pepper if needed.

4. Ladle the soup into mugs or bowls, dust with the remaining grated Parmesan, and serve.

TO GO: This soup is best made at the last minute. Pack the eggs, grated cheese, and spinach separately and bring them to the party with your pot of chicken stock, a bowl, and a whisk. At the party, while the soup is reheating, whisk the eggs and ½ cup [40 g] of the cheese in your bowl and season with salt and pepper. Finish the soup off as directed and serve.

SOPA DE LIMA

MAKES 8 TO 10 TASTING PORTIONS OR 6 FULL SERVINGS

I've been a huge fan of this lime, chicken, and tortilla soup from the very first bowl I sampled on the Yucatán Peninsula of Mexico many years ago. You can cut corners and use canned chicken stock, a rotisserie-roasted chicken from your favorite market, and a bag of tortilla chips; but let me tell you, it won't be the same. Serve with Citrus Salad with Crème Fraîche and Tarragon (page 159).

TORTILLA STRIPS

Canola oil for frying

6 corn tortillas, about 5½ in [14 cm] in diameter, cut into ½-in- [12-mm-] thick strips

Sea salt

SOUP

2 Tbsp olive oil

1 large onion, chopped

3 garlic cloves, finely chopped

Sea salt

Freshly ground black pepper

1 jalapeño chile, cored, seeded, and finely chopped, plus more as needed

1 cup [240 g] diced tomatoes, fresh or canned

1 Tbsp chopped fresh oregano

4 cups [960 ml] Roasted Chicken Stock (page 30) or canned low-sodium broth

1 cup [110 g] cooked shredded chicken

¼ cup [60 ml] fresh lime juice, plus more as needed

GARNISHES

1 poblano chile, seeded and chopped

1 ripe but not overly ripe or mushy avocado, cut into ½-in [12-mm] cubes

¼ cup [10 g] finely chopped fresh cilantro

1 cup [80 g] cotija Mexican cheese or feta, grated or finely chopped

1 lime, cut into wedges

1. **TO MAKE THE TORTILLA STRIPS:** In a medium skillet over medium-high heat, add enough canola oil to reach a depth of ½ in [12 mm] and heat until a small piece of tortilla or a speck of salt immediately sizzles on contact. Cook the tortillas, one at a time, for 1 to 2 minutes on each side, or until golden brown and slightly puffed. Using tongs, transfer the tortillas to paper towels to drain; sprinkle with salt.

2. **TO MAKE THE SOUP:** In a large stockpot over low heat, warm the olive oil. Add the onion and garlic and cook for 10 minutes. Season with salt and pepper, stir in the jalapeño, and cook for another 2 minutes. Stir in the tomatoes and oregano and cook for 5 minutes more. Turn the heat to high, add the chicken stock, and bring to a boil. Turn the heat to low, cover, and cook for 30 minutes. Add the chicken and cook for another 5 minutes.

3. Just before serving, add the lime juice to the soup. Taste and adjust the seasoning, adding more salt, pepper, jalapeño, or lime juice if needed.

4. Ladle the soup into mugs or bowls, top each with two or three tortilla strips, and serve. Have all the garnishes arranged decoratively on a large serving plate and let guests add their own.

TO GO: Pack the tortilla strips and garnishes separately.

CHICKEN, CHARRED TOMATO, AND CHILE POSOLE

MAKES 10 TO 12 TASTING PORTIONS OR 8 FULL SERVINGS

Posole is a hearty Mexican stew made with hominy (white corn kernels soaked in a lye or lime bath to soften the outer hull), chile peppers, tomatoes, beans, and shredded chicken. It requires several steps but is one of those soups that are easy to put together since most of the work can be done ahead of time. You'll need to soak the hominy and the beans overnight in a pot of cold water and then simmer them the next day. You can use canned hominy, but it doesn't have the same texture or flavor. If you make Roasted Chicken Stock, you'll have homemade stock *and* chicken to use for this soup.

Served with all kinds of fun garnishes—cubed avocado, chopped cilantro, sour cream, warm corn tortillas, and lime wedges—posole is ideal for parties.

HOMINY AND BEANS

1½ cups [340 g] prepared white hominy

1½ cups [340 g] dried pinto, cranberry, Jacob's cattle, or other hearty dried beans

¼ large white onion

Sea salt

6 peppercorns

1 bay leaf

CHARRED TOMATO AND CHILE SAUCE

6 dry guajillo or New Mexican chiles, stemmed, halved lengthwise, and seeded

2 large tomatoes

SOUP

3 Tbsp olive oil

1 medium white onion, thinly sliced

2 large garlic cloves, thinly sliced

½ cup [120 g] crushed canned tomatoes with their juice

2½ tsp dried Mexican oregano or regular oregano or 2 Tbsp chopped fresh oregano

Sea salt

Freshly ground black pepper

8 cups [2 L] Roasted Chicken Stock (page 30) or canned low-sodium broth

4 cups [430 g] shredded cooked chicken (from the Roasted Chicken Stock or other roasted chicken)

GARNISHES

1 ripe but not mushy avocado, cut into ½-in [12-mm] cubes

½ cup [30 g] packed chopped fresh cilantro

1 lime, cut into 8 wedges

1 cup [190 g] sour cream

Quick Pickled Radishes (page 171)

8 corn tortillas, warmed, or corn tortilla strips (see page 87)

continued

1. **TO MAKE THE HOMINY AND BEANS:** Place the hominy in a large bowl, add enough cold water to cover by 3 in [7.5 cm], and soak overnight. Place the beans in a second large bowl, add enough cold water to cover by 3 in [7.5 cm], and soak overnight.

2. Drain the hominy and transfer to a large stockpot. Add enough fresh cold water to cover by 3 in [7.5 cm] and bring to a boil over high heat. Turn the heat to low, add the onion, and simmer gently for 1½ to 2 hours, until the hominy "pops" or begins to open like a flower. Once the hominy is tender but not soft, transfer it to a colander and drain it over a clean bowl; reserve the cooking water.

3. Meanwhile, drain the beans and transfer them to a second stockpot. Add enough fresh cold water to cover and season with salt. Add the peppercorns and bay leaf and bring to a boil over high heat. Turn the heat to low and simmer gently for about 30 minutes, or until just tender. Drain the beans and discard the bay leaf. Set aside.

4. **TO MAKE THE SAUCE:** Preheat a cast-iron skillet or griddle over high heat. Working with one chile strip at a time, and using tongs, cook the strips for about 30 seconds per side, or until they just start to smoke. Be careful not to overcook them, or they will become bitter. Transfer the chile strips to a bowl, add enough boiling water to cover, and let soak for 30 minutes.

5. Meanwhile, preheat the broiler. Place the tomatoes on a rimmed baking sheet and broil, flipping them from side to side, for about 8 minutes, or until the skin is almost totally blackened on all sides. Transfer to a plate and let cool. Core the tomato.

6. Drain the chiles, reserving the soaking water. In a blender, combine the soaked chile strips, ½ cup [120 ml] of the reserved soaking water, and the tomatoes and purée. Set aside. (You can make 1 day ahead. Cover tightly and refrigerate.)

7. **TO MAKE THE SOUP:** In a large stockpot over medium-low heat, warm the olive oil. Add the onion and garlic and cook, stirring, for 8 minutes, without letting them brown. Add the crushed tomatoes, oregano, and reserved tomato-chile sauce; season with salt and pepper; and cook, stirring, for about 3 minutes. Add the cooked hominy and 2 cups [480 ml] of the reserved hominy cooking liquid. Add the chicken stock and bring to a boil over high heat. Turn the heat to medium-low, add the cooked beans, and simmer gently for about 45 minutes. Add the shredded chicken and simmer for another 5 to 15 minutes, or until slightly thickened. Taste and adjust the seasoning, adding more salt and pepper if needed.

8. Ladle the soup into mugs or bowls and serve along with any or all of the garnishes.

TO GO: Pack the tortillas and the garnishes separately on a baking sheet. At the party, warm the tortillas in a 300°F [150°C] oven.

What to Do with Leftover Chicken (and Meat) from Homemade Stock?

When you're making stock from beef bones or a whole chicken, you can end up with a lot of leftover meat. Other than using the poultry and meat in a soup, here are some creative ways to make the most of your leftovers.

- Make chicken salad with fresh dill or tarragon, chopped scallions, lemon juice, and a touch of mayonnaise.

- Use leftover chicken or beef to make a potpie or shepherd's pie.

- Add leftover chicken, fresh spinach leaves or chopped chard or kale, and cooked rice to chicken stock to create a quick soup.

- Make chicken or beef tacos and serve with Quick Pickled Radishes (page 171).

- Make chicken or beef enchiladas.

- Make chicken or beef hash with cubed cooked potatoes, bell peppers, and onions and top with poached eggs and hot sauce.

- Make a chopped salad with shredded chicken, lettuce, olives, feta, cherry tomatoes, sweet peppers, chopped hard-boiled egg, and any other vegetables you have on hand.

- Make a chicken, bacon, lettuce, and avocado sandwich on whole-wheat toast with tarragon mayonnaise.

- Make an Asian-style chicken salad with thinly sliced napa cabbage, roasted peanuts, lime juice, fish sauce, canola oil, and chopped fresh coriander and mint.

- Add leftover chicken or beef to a risotto or a tomato-based pasta sauce.

- Make a chicken or beef curry.

CHICKEN SOUP
WITH NOODLES AND MATZO BALLS

DF

MAKES 14 TO 16 TASTING PORTIONS OR 12 FULL SERVINGS

"Jewish penicillin" was what we always called the rich chicken soup we were served as kids growing up in New York. It's what we ate whenever one of us had a cold or the flu. This is the most basic of recipes, but there are several ways to serve it. You can cut the vegetables and chicken into big chunks to give the soup a rustic feel, or you can cut them into small, even shapes and give your soup a simple elegance. For a hearty soup, you can serve the matzo balls and noodles together. Always slightly undercook the noodles separately (see page 97) until they are al dente, or still have a bite, and then add them to the soup to finish cooking.

Matzo balls are the classic accompaniment to chicken soup during Passover, or *Pesach*, but they are a treat any time of year. Plan on letting the matzo ball mixture sit for about 2 hours, covered and refrigerated, before cooking. Seltzer water gives the balls a fluffy consistency. And be sure to use the fat skimmed off the chicken stock.

MATZO BALLS

4 eggs

4 Tbsp [60 ml] melted chicken fat or canola oil

½ cup [120 ml] seltzer water

½ cup [120 ml] Roasted Chicken Stock (page 30)

Sea salt

Freshly ground black pepper

1 cup [120 g] matzo meal

SOUP

12 cups [2.8 L] Roasted Chicken Stock (page 30)

1 medium onion, chopped

4 large celery stalks, chopped

2 large or 4 medium carrots, peeled and chopped

½ cup [30 g] packed finely chopped fresh parsley

Sea salt

Freshly ground black pepper

9½ oz [270 g] cooked chicken, skinned and shredded or cut into small pieces

10 oz [280 g] vermicelli or egg noodles

¼ cup [15 g] packed finely chopped fresh dill (optional)

1. **TO MAKE THE MATZO BALLS:** In a large bowl, vigorously whisk the eggs. Whisk in the chicken fat, seltzer water, and chicken stock and season with salt and pepper. Add the matzo meal and stir to form a smooth batter. Cover and refrigerate for at least 2 hours, or up to overnight.

2. Bring a large pot of salted water to a boil over high heat. Remove the matzo batter from the refrigerator. Using your hands (if you wet them, it will be easier to work with the batter), form 12 medium matzo balls or 14 to 16 smaller balls. Add the balls to the boiling water and turn the heat to medium-low. Cover and cook for about 25 minutes.

3. **TO MAKE THE SOUP:** In a large stockpot over medium-high heat, warm the chicken stock. Add the onion, celery, carrots, and ¼ cup [15 g] of the parsley; season with salt and pepper; and bring to a boil over high heat. Turn the heat to low, partially cover, and simmer for 15 minutes. Add the chicken and simmer for another 5 minutes.

4. Meanwhile, bring another large pot of salted water to a boil over high heat. Add the noodles and cook until almost cooked through (al dente) but not quite soft. Drain the noodles.

5. At this point, the matzo balls should be soft and almost completely cooked through. With a slotted spoon, drain the balls thoroughly, add them to the soup, and continue cooking for another 5 minutes. Add the noodles to the soup and cook for another 5 to 7 minutes, or until the matzo balls are soft, the noodles are tender, and the vegetables are cooked. Taste and adjust the seasoning, adding more salt and pepper if needed.

6. Ladle the soup into mugs or bowls, sprinkle with the remaining ¼ cup [15 g] parsley and the dill, if desired, and serve.

TO GO: Cook the pasta until al dente, drain it, and add it to the cooled soup. Cook the matzo balls for only 20 minutes, drain them, and add them to the soup off the heat. Bring the remaining parsley and the dill in a separate container. At the party, reheat the soup; the matzo balls and noodles will finish cooking while the soup heats up. Sprinkle each bowl with the parsley and dill.

THAI RED CURRY– CHICKEN NOODLE SOUP

MAKES 10 TO 12 TASTING PORTIONS OR 8 FULL SERVINGS

This Thai version of chicken noodle soup is fragrant with coconut milk, garlic, ginger, cilantro, scallions, spices, and red curry paste. Cooked chicken, udon noodles, and fresh spinach and snow peas are added just before serving. Last-minute garnishes include grated carrots, bean sprouts, cilantro, and scallions. This is a hearty, main-course kind of soup. Serve it with Citrus Salad with Crème Fraîche and Tarragon (page 159).

4 Tbsp [60 ml] canola oil

6 shallots, very thinly sliced

Sea salt

Freshly ground black pepper

4 garlic cloves, very thinly sliced

4 scallions, very thinly sliced

One 2-in [5-cm] piece fresh ginger, grated on a Microplane or the smallest holes of a box grater

2 tsp Madras curry powder

½ tsp ground turmeric

2 Tbsp red curry paste

½ cup [30 g] packed finely chopped fresh cilantro with stems

8 cups [2 L] Basic Chicken Stock (page 29) or Roasted Chicken Stock (page 30)

One 13½-oz [40-ml] can unsweetened coconut milk

2 Tbsp fish sauce (*nam pla*)

2 Tbsp soy sauce or tamari

2 cups [215 g] shredded cooked chicken

8 oz [230 g] udon noodles

6 oz [170 g] snow peas, halved lengthwise

10 oz [280 g] baby spinach or finely chopped mustard greens

GARNISHES

2 medium carrots, peeled and shredded on the largest holes of a box grater

1 cup [230 g] bean sprouts

½ cup [30 g] packed chopped fresh cilantro

3 scallions, very finely chopped

2 Tbsp Chinese chili paste or hot-pepper sauce

1. In a large stockpot over medium-high heat, warm 2 Tbsp of the canola oil. Add the shallots, season with salt and pepper, and cook, stirring, for 10 to 15 minutes, or until they begin to turn brown and seem to be on the verge of burning. Using a slotted spoon, transfer the cooked shallots to a small bowl and set aside.

2. Turn the heat to low; add the remaining 2 Tbsp canola oil, the garlic, scallions, and ginger; and cook for 2 minutes. Add half the cooked shallots, the curry powder, turmeric, and red curry paste and cook, stirring, for another 2 minutes. Add the cilantro, season with salt and pepper, and cook for 1 minute more. Turn the heat to high, add the chicken stock, and bring to a boil. Turn the heat to low; add the coconut milk, fish sauce, and soy sauce; and cook, partially covered, for 5 minutes. Taste and adjust the seasoning, adding more

continued

salt and pepper, if needed. Add the cooked chicken. (At this point, you can transfer the soup to an airtight container and refrigerate for up to 1 day.)

3. Bring a large pot of salted water to a boil over high heat. Add the noodles and cook for 10 minutes, or until almost tender. Drain.

4. Turn the heat under the soup to medium-low and bring to a gentle simmer. Add the peas and spinach and then remove from the heat.

5. Divide the noodles among mugs or bowls. Ladle equal portions of the soup, vegetables, and chicken over them. Sprinkle with any or all of the garnishes and serve.

TO GO: Make the soup up to the addition of the chicken and remove it from the heat. Cook the noodles for 9 minutes, drain, and let cool. Toss the noodles with about ¼ cup [60 ml] cold water (to keep them from clumping up) and pack them in a container. Pack the raw spinach, peas, and garnishes separately. At the party, reheat the soup; drain the noodles and add with the vegetables just before serving. The heat of the soup will finish cooking the noodles.

Cook Those Noodles Separately, Please!

In *almost* all cases it's best to cook pasta, noodles, and rice separately and then add it to your soup. The reason is simple. When pasta or rice cooks, it soaks up the liquid it's being cooked in. If you cook the pasta or rice in your soup, you will end up with a thick, stewlike mess. All your gorgeous broth will have been "drunk" by your pasta. There are a few exceptions to this; such as when you do want a thick, stewlike soup, like Yia Yia's Greek Avgole-mono (page 84).

Here's my advice: Cook noodles and rice in a separate pot but just slightly undercook them. The reason? Noodles and rice will continue to cook when you add them to your hot soup, and you don't want them to overcook. I generally cut down the cooking time by 3 to 5 minutes. For pasta and noodles, that means you are looking for a true al dente consistency; pasta with a real bite. It will soften when added to your soup without soaking up all the broth. The same treatment also works for rice. Remove it when it still has a bit of a bite, let it cool down a bit, and then add it to the soup.

The only time I cook pasta directly in a soup is when I'm working with very tiny pasta, like pastina, *ditalini*, or *acini di pepe.* Anything bigger—including orzo—should be cooked separately.

GREEK-STYLE TURKEY AND RICE SOUP

WITH MEYER LEMON AND DILL

MAKES 12 TO 14 TASTING PORTIONS OR 8 TO 10 FULL SERVINGS

GF

I was visiting an old friend in Northern California whose neighbor had Meyer lemon trees that were dripping with bright fruit. I set out to make a version of the classic Greek lemon-rice soup (*avgolemono*) using leftover turkey stock, turkey meat (from our Thanksgiving bird), cooked rice, and the distinctively sweet orange-lemon flavor of Meyer lemons.

If you don't have access to Meyer lemons, use regular lemons, but try to find at least one Meyer lemon for the garnish. The amount of cream you add depends on how creamy you like your soup. Start with ⅓ cup [80 ml] and then add more. Serve with Mixed Greens Salad with Mint-Tangerine Vinaigrette (page 156).

1½ Tbsp olive oil

1 medium onion, chopped

1 medium parsnip, peeled and chopped

1 medium carrot, peeled and chopped

Sea salt

Freshly ground black pepper

8 cups [2 L] "Recycled" Chicken or Turkey Stock (page 31)

2½ cups [270 g] cooked, skinless, cubed or shredded turkey or chicken

2 egg yolks

⅓ to ½ cup [80 to 120 ml] heavy cream

¼ to ½ cup [60 to 120 ml] fresh Meyer lemon juice or regular lemon juice (see headnote), ½ tsp freshly grated Meyer lemon or regular lemon zest, plus 8 to 10 paper-thin slices of Meyer lemon or regular lemon, seeded

1½ Tbsp chopped fresh dill, plus ¼ cup [15 g]

1 cup [200 g] cooked white rice

¼ cup [15 g] packed chopped fresh parsley

1. In a large stockpot over low heat, warm the olive oil. Add the onion and cook, stirring, for 5 minutes. Add the parsnip and carrot, season with salt and pepper, and cook, stirring once or twice, for another 5 minutes. Turn the heat to high, add the stock, and bring to a boil. Turn the heat to low, cover, and simmer for 20 minutes. Add the turkey and stir.

2. In a small bowl, whisk the egg yolks and the cream until blended. Ladle about ½ cup [120 ml] of the hot soup into the yolk-cream mixture and whisk until blended. (This step is called *tempering*, and it helps introduce a cold liquid to a hot liquid and at the same time prevent the mixture from curdling.) Add the yolk-cream mixture to the soup and simmer, whisking, until smooth and fully incorporated. Add the lemon juice, lemon zest, and 1½ Tbsp dill and season with salt and pepper. The soup should have a distinct lemon flavor. Stir in the cooked rice, being careful not to let it clump up.

3. Simmer the soup over low heat for about 10 minutes, until hot and slightly thickened. The rice will soak up some of the stock, so you don't want to let it cook too long in the hot soup. Taste and adjust the seasoning, adding more salt and pepper if needed.

4. In a small bowl, using a fork, gently toss the remaining ¼ cup [15 g] dill with the parsley.

5. Ladle the soup into mugs or bowls, top each with a sprinkling of the dill-parsley mixture, and serve with the lemon slices.

TO GO: Pack the soup and the rice separately. Pack the herbs and lemon slices separately. At the party stir the rice into the reheated soup to prevent it from clumping. Add the herbs and lemon slices just before serving.

MEAT SOUPS

When it's cold out (I'm talking bone-chilling I-can't-get-warm kind of cold), there's nothing quite like a meat-based soup to warm you up. Meat plays an important role in all these soups, but it's not necessarily the star. Black Bean and Chorizo Soup is filled with bits of spicy chorizo sausage, but it's also thick with onions, beans, and spices and is served with avocado crema and pickled radish topping. And Italian Wedding Soup, while chock-full of Swiss chard, carrots, celery, onions, tomatoes, and fresh herbs, really gets its distinct flavor from beef-and-pork meatballs flavored with Parmesan cheese and fresh basil. The goal is meat in moderation, even in your soup.

MAYA'S HOT-AND-SOUR BROTH
WITH BEEF-AND-PORK WONTONS

MAKES 12 TO 14 TASTING PORTIONS OR 8 FULL SERVINGS

When is a soup a broth? Generally it's a matter of semantics. This version, a thin, spicy chicken broth chock-full of meaty wontons, comes from my daughter Maya who has lived in Beijing for several years. In her version, ground beef and pork are mixed with ginger and garlic and packed inside wonton wrappers. The broth gets its special sour flavor from Chinese black vinegar, which is available in any Asian market. In fact, many of the ingredients used here can be found in Asian food shops or in the Asian food aisle of your supermarket. You can also cook the dumplings and serve any extras on the side with a simple dipping sauce of soy sauce, a drop of sesame oil, chili paste, chopped scallions, and fresh cilantro.

BEEF-AND-PORK WONTONS

1 garlic clove, minced

1 scallion, finely chopped

One 1-in [2.5-cm] piece fresh ginger, peeled and minced

½ tsp sesame oil

8 oz [230 g] ground beef

8 oz [230 g] ground pork

½ tsp Chinese chili paste with garlic

1 tsp Chinese black vinegar

Pinch of sea salt

48 wonton wrappers

SOUP

1½ Tbsp canola oil

3 garlic cloves; 2 thinly sliced, 1 quartered

1 Tbsp finely minced fresh ginger

2 scallions, chopped

1½ tsp sesame oil

⅓ cup [80 ml] Chinese black vinegar

1 tsp Lao Gan Ma (spicy chili crisp sauce) or Chinese chili paste (optional)

8 cups [2 L] Basic Chicken Stock (page 29) or canned low-sodium broth

¼ to 1 tsp Sriracha or other hot-pepper sauce

½ cup [30 g] packed finely chopped fresh cilantro

||||||||||||||||||||||||||||

1. **TO MAKE THE WONTONS:** In a large bowl, combine the garlic, scallion, ginger, sesame oil, ground beef, ground pork, chili paste, vinegar, and salt. Using your hands or a rubber spatula, mix thoroughly to make sure that all the ingredients are evenly incorporated.

2. Have a small bowl of water at hand. Fill the center of a wonton wrapper with a heaping 1 tsp of the filling. Dab your finger in the water and moisten the edge of the wrapper. Fold the wonton wrapper over to form a triangle and press the edges together with your fingers to seal it well. Repeat with the remaining wrappers and filling. You should have enough filling for 48 wontons, give or take a few not-so-pretty ones. Arrange the wontons about 1 in [2.5 cm] apart on a parchment paper-lined baking sheet; the wontons can be covered and refrigerated for up to 3 hours.

continued

3. **TO MAKE THE SOUP:** In a large stockpot over low heat, warm the canola oil. Add all the garlic, the ginger, and scallions and cook, stirring, for 3 minutes. Stir in the sesame oil, vinegar, and Lao Gan Ma (if using) and cook for 1 minute. Turn the heat to high, add the chicken stock, and bring to a boil. Turn the heat to low and add ¼ tsp of the Sriracha and ¼ cup [15 g] of the cilantro. Taste and adjust the seasoning, adding more Sriracha if you like a spicy broth. Cover and simmer for about 20 minutes.

4. Meanwhile, fill a large pot a little over halfway with water and bring to a boil over high heat. Add half the wontons to the water and return to a boil. Add 1 cup [240 ml] cold water and return to a boil. Add another 1 cup [240 ml] cold water and bring to a boil. Using a slotted spoon, transfer the wontons to a clean parchment paper–lined baking sheet. Repeat with the remaining wontons.

5. Ladle the soup into mugs or small bowls. Add three or four dumplings to each tasting-size portion, or six dumplings to each full-size portion, sprinkle with the remaining ¼ cup [15 g] cilantro, and serve.

TO GO: Place the cooked, cooled wontons in a glass or plastic container with about 1 cup [240 ml] of the cooled broth. Cover and refrigerate. Pack the remaining ¼ cup [15 g] cilantro in a separate container. At the party, reheat the soup. Add the wontons and cook for about 5 minutes, or until hot.

PASTA E FAGIOLI

MAKES 10 TO 12 TASTING PORTIONS OR 8 FULL SERVINGS

Italy's traditional pasta and bean soup is simple and satisfying. In this version, the stock is scented with fresh rosemary, generous chunks of cubed boneless pork loin roast, white beans, garlic, tomatoes, and a small shaped pasta. You can also substitute 8 oz [230 g] thick-cut bacon, cut into ½-in [12-mm] pieces for the pork loin (see Note). It's a thick, hearty, main-course soup. Serve it with warm, crusty bread.

NOTE: *If substituting bacon for the pork loin, add the bacon to the stockpot and cook over medium-low heat, stirring occasionally, for 8 to 10 minutes, until the bacon is crisp. Pour off all but 1 Tbsp of the bacon fat. Add 1 tsp flour to the fat and whisk over low heat for 2 minutes. Then proceed as directed.*

2 Tbsp all-purpose flour

Sea salt

Freshly ground pepper

12 oz [340 g] boneless pork loin roast, cut into ½-in [12-mm] cubes

3 Tbsp olive oil

1 cup [240 ml] dry white wine

1 small onion, diced

6 garlic cloves, coarsely chopped

2 medium carrots, peeled and diced

2 medium celery stalks, diced

¼ cup [15 g] packed chopped fresh parsley leaves

2 tsp chopped fresh rosemary leaves

6 cups [1.4 L] Basic Chicken Stock (page 29), Roasted Chicken Stock (page 30), or canned low-sodium broth

One 28-oz [750-g] can crushed tomatoes

¾ cup [90 g] small pasta (*conchigliette*, ditalini, *tubetti*, or orzo work well)

4 cups [880 g] cooked white cannellini beans (see page 107) or canned beans (drained, rinsed, and re-drained)

Dash of hot-pepper sauce (optional)

1 cup [80 g] freshly grated Parmesan cheese

Parsley Pesto (page 165) for garnish

8 Double-Cheese Croutes (page 168; optional)

1. Spoon the flour into a shallow bowl or pie plate and season with salt and pepper. Lightly coat all sides of the pork with the seasoned flour.

2. Heat a large stockpot over medium-high heat until hot but not smoking, then add 2 Tbsp of the olive oil. Working in batches to avoid crowding the pan, cook the pork, stirring occasionally, for about 5 minutes per batch, until browned. Using a slotted spoon, transfer the browned pork to a bowl.

3. Add the wine to the pot, turn the heat to high, and simmer, stirring with a wooden spoon to release any bits clinging to the bottom of the pot, for 2 minutes. Pour the wine mixture into the bowl with the cooked pork and set aside.

4. Turn the heat to low and add the remaining 1 Tbsp olive oil. Add the onion and garlic and cook, stirring, for about 3 minutes, until the onion begins to soften. Add the carrots, celery, 2 Tbsp of the parsley, and 1 tsp of the rosemary; season with salt and pepper; and cook, stirring occasionally,

continued

for another 3 minutes. Add the chicken stock and tomatoes, turn the heat to high, and bring the mixture to a boil. Stir in the pasta, beans, and browned pork with all its juices and cook, partially covered, for 10 to 12 minutes more. Taste and adjust the seasoning, adding more salt and pepper if needed. The soup is ready when the pork is tender and the pasta is just cooked through, still al dente. Just before serving, stir in the remaining 2 Tbsp parsley, 1 tsp rosemary, and the hot-pepper sauce (if using).

5. Ladle the soup into mugs or bowls; top with Parmesan, a dollop of pesto, and a cheese croute, if desired; and serve.

TO GO: Remove the soup from the heat as soon as you add the pasta, beans, and pork. Pack the pesto, cheese, and croutes separately. At the party, reheat the soup for 10 to 12 minutes, until the pasta is just tender.

Canned Beans or Fresh?

Opening a can of beans is a whole lot faster than cooking up a fresh batch. But it always tastes a little . . . metallic. If you choose to use canned beans in any of these soup recipes be sure to drain the beans in a sieve or colander, rinse them under cold running water for a full minute, and then drain and dry thoroughly.

The main advantage of cooking beans from scratch is that you can control the texture—as opposed to canned beans, which are almost always overcooked and mushy. To cook beans from scratch, soak the dried beans in a bowl of cold water for at least 2 hours, or up to overnight. Drain, transfer to a large stockpot, and add enough fresh cold water to cover them. You can add a quartered onion, bay leaf, sea salt, and pepper if you wish. Bring to a boil over high heat, turn the heat to low, and cook, partially covered, for about 1 hour, depending on the type of bean, until almost tender. The beans should retain their shape and still have a bite, that is, not overly soft and mushy.

If you want to cook dried beans but forgot to soak them overnight, here's a quick method. Rinse the beans under cold water and drain them. Transfer the beans to a large stockpot, add enough cold water to cover them by about 2 in [5 cm], and bring to a boil over high heat. As soon as the water boils, remove the pot from the heat, cover, and set aside for 1 hour. Then proceed with the recipe, cooking the beans until almost tender.

PORTUGUESE-STYLE KALE, WHITE BEAN, AND CHORIZO SOUP

GF

MAKES 12 TO 14 TASTING PORTIONS OR 8 FULL SERVINGS

Years ago, I traveled through the fertile Alentejo region of Portugal, where kale grows in abundance. It came as no surprise, then, that I encountered some version of this soup almost everywhere I went. My favorite among them featured buttery white beans, potatoes, and spicy chorizo sausage. It is a full-flavored soup that is hearty enough to make a whole meal. Look for fresh green kale, Tuscan kale, dinosaur kale, or Lacinato kale (also called *cavolo nero*) at your local farmers' market. If you can't find chorizo or if the chorizo you find isn't very spicy, substitute hot Italian sausage and add a dash of hot-pepper sauce and paprika, or a pinch of red chili flakes. Serve with warm crusty bread or Buttery Biscuits (page 155).

12 oz [340 g] fresh chorizo sausage

1 large leek

1½ Tbsp olive oil

3 garlic cloves, chopped or thinly sliced

8 oz [230 g] potato, such as Yukon gold, peeled and cut into ½-in [12-mm] pieces

1 large bunch kale, center ribs and stems removed, coarsely chopped

8 cups [2 L] Basic Chicken Stock (page 29) or Vegetable Stock (page 34)

3 cups [660 g] cooked white cannellini beans (see page 107) or canned beans (drained, rinsed, and re-drained)

Sea salt

Freshly ground black pepper

Pinch of red chili flakes (optional)

GARNISHES

½ cup [30 g] packed chopped fresh parsley

8 paper-thin lemon slices

½ cup [40 g] freshly grated Parmesan cheese

|||||||||||||||||||||||||||

1. Cut one third of the chorizo sausage crosswise into thin slices and reserve. Remove the casings from the remaining chorizo and crumble the sausage. Trim off the dark green sections from the leek and save for making vegetable stock. Halve the pale green and white section lengthwise. Rinse under cold running water, pat dry, and cut crosswise into ½-in [12-mm] pieces.

2. In a large stockpot over medium heat, warm 1 Tbsp of the olive oil. Add the crumbled sausage and cook, stirring occasionally, for 5 minutes, or until lightly browned. Turn the heat to low, add the leek and garlic, and cook for another 5 minutes. Add the potato and cook, stirring, for 2 minutes more. Stir in the kale and cook another minute or two to make sure all the ingredients are evenly incorporated. Turn the heat to high, add the chicken stock, and bring to a boil. Turn the heat to low, add the beans, and season with salt and pepper. Stir the pot and simmer, covered, for 15 minutes.

3. Meanwhile, in a medium skillet over medium heat, warm the remaining ½ Tbsp olive oil. Add the sliced chorizo and cook for about 3 minutes, until well browned on both sides. Using a slotted spoon, transfer the sausage to paper towels to drain. Then transfer the drained sausage to the stockpot and simmer the soup for another 15 to 20 minutes. Taste and adjust the seasoning, adding more salt and pepper or the red chili flakes if needed.

4. Ladle the soup into mugs or bowls and serve with any or all of the garnishes.

TO GO: Pack all the garnishes separately.

HOPE'S ITALIAN SAUSAGE-ZUCCHINI SOUP

MAKES 10 TO 12 TASTING PORTIONS OR 8 FULL SERVINGS

The recipe for this hearty soup originally came from my friend Hope Murphy's mother, Carol, who discovered it decades ago in the food section of the Springfield, Massachusetts, newspaper, *The Republican*. Hope has adapted it over the years into a lighter soup. Serve with Crostada with Butternut, Red Onion, and Feta (page 153).

3 Tbsp olive oil

8 oz [230 g] sweet Italian turkey or pork sausage, casings removed

8 oz [230 g] spicy Italian turkey or pork sausage, casings removed

1 small onion, diced

2 large garlic cloves, minced

Sea salt

Freshly ground black pepper

Two 28-oz [794-g] cans whole tomatoes, coarsely chopped, with their juices

2 Tbsp packed mixture of chopped fresh basil, oregano, and parsley, plus ½ cup [30 g]

1 tsp granulated sugar

2 lb [910 g] zucchini, halved lengthwise and cut crosswise into ½-in [12-mm] slices

3 large celery stalks, diced

1 large green bell pepper, deribbed, seeded, and diced

2 cups [480 ml] Basic Chicken Stock (page 29) or canned low-sodium broth

Pinch of red chili flakes (optional)

½ cup [40 g] freshly grated Parmesan cheese

1. In a large stockpot over medium heat, warm the olive oil. Add all the sausage and cook, stirring and breaking it up, for 6 to 8 minutes, or until just brown. (If there is a lot of grease, remove all but 1 Tbsp of it.) Add the onion and garlic, season with salt and pepper, and cook, stirring, for 1 minute. Add the tomatoes, 2 Tbsp herb mixture, and sugar and simmer, covered, for 20 minutes.

2. Add the zucchini, celery, bell pepper, chicken stock, and red chili flakes (if using). Raise the heat to bring to a boil, then lower the heat and simmer for 15 to 20 minutes, until the vegetables are tender. Taste and adjust the seasoning, adding more salt and pepper if needed.

3. Ladle the soup into mugs or bowls, garnish with a sprinkling of grated Parmesan and the remaining herb mixture, and serve.

TO GO: Pack the grated cheese and chopped herbs separately.

National Soup Swap Day—No Kidding

There's a holiday for just about everything. It seems that every day of the year is devoted to some strange passion: National Pie Day, National Ice Cream Day, National Cat Day, National Naked Gardening Day. Yup, I'm not making this stuff up. Go on. Google it if you don't believe me. Lo and behold, there is also something called Soup Swap Day!

National Soup Swap Day is held on the third Saturday in January. It began in 2006 in a Seattle kitchen, and it turns out that many people around the country are making soup and sharing it with friends, colleagues, and neighbors.

The idea is pretty much the same as the one that is the basis of this book: Make a big pot of soup, have a party, and divvy up the soup leftovers for everyone to take home. Good to know that there's a whole day devoted to this soup-swap idea. But I say why devote a single day when you can devote an entire winter to making and swapping soups.

SAUSAGE, CABBAGE, AND ROOT VEGETABLE SOUP

MAKES 12 TO 14 TASTING PORTIONS OR 8 FULL PORTIONS

This is an adaptation of a soup I created for my James Beard Award–winning article on cabbage for *Eating Well* magazine. For this French-style soup, sausage, cabbage, and root vegetables are simmered together to make a comforting and healthful meal. Serve the soup piping hot topped with grated Parmesan cheese. Like most soups, it is even more flavorful if it's made a day ahead. Serve with Skillet Corn Bread with Chive and Brown Butter (page 154).

2 Tbsp extra-virgin olive oil

1 lb [455 g] mild or spicy Italian turkey sausage or pork sausage, casings removed

1 medium onion, chopped

3 garlic cloves, thinly sliced

Sea salt

Freshly ground black pepper

2 medium carrots, peeled and cut crosswise into ½-in [12-mm] pieces

2 small turnips, peeled and cut into ½-in [12-mm] pieces

1 medium celery root, peeled and cut into ½-in [12-mm] pieces

8 oz [230 g] Yukon gold potato, peeled and cut into ½-in [12-mm] pieces

½ medium head green cabbage, very thinly sliced

8 cups [2 L] Basic Chicken Stock (page 29), Roasted Chicken Stock (page 30), or canned low-sodium broth

¾ cup [180 ml] dry white wine

1 medium tomato, chopped

1 Tbsp chopped fresh rosemary

1 Tbsp chopped fresh thyme

½ cup [40 g] freshly grated Parmesan cheese

1. In a large stockpot over medium-high heat, warm 1 Tbsp of the olive oil. Add the sausage and cook, stirring and breaking it up, for about 10 minutes, until well browned. Using a slotted spoon, transfer the sausage to paper towels to drain.

2. Turn the heat to medium; add the remaining 1 Tbsp olive oil, the onion, and garlic to the pot; and season with salt and pepper. Cook, stirring, for 2 to 3 minutes, until the onion begins to soften. Add the carrots, turnips, celery root, and potato and cook, stirring once or twice, for 4 to 5 minutes, or until the vegetables are almost tender. Add the cabbage and cook for about 2 minutes, just until the cabbage begins to wilt. Return the sausage to the pot; add the chicken stock, wine, tomato, rosemary, and thyme; and stir. Turn the heat to high and bring to a boil. Turn the heat to low and simmer, covered, for 1 hour.

3. Remove the lid and simmer for about 15 minutes, until the stock is reduced and the flavor more assertive. Taste and adjust the seasoning, adding more salt and pepper if needed.

4. Ladle the soup into mugs or bowls and serve topped with the Parmesan.

TO GO: Pack the grated cheese separately.

BLACK BEAN AND CHORIZO SOUP
WITH AVOCADO CREMA

MAKES 10 TO 12 TASTING PORTIONS OR 6 TO 8 FULL SERVINGS

Infused with ground cumin and slightly spicy Spanish chorizo, this soup is full of bold flavors. I serve it with an avocado crema and the quickest pickled radishes you've ever made. Skillet Corn Bread with Chive and Brown Butter (page 154) and Citrus Salad with Crème Fraîche and Tarragon (page 159) would be excellent accompaniments. The beans need to soak overnight, so plan accordingly.

2 cups [440 g] dried black beans
1 bay leaf
1 small onion, quartered, plus
    2 medium onions, finely chopped
6 peppercorns
Sprig of fresh thyme
Sprig of fresh parsley
Sea salt
1½ Tbsp olive oil
3 oz [85 g] Spanish-style chorizo (not
    soft fresh chorizo), finely chopped
2 garlic cloves, finely chopped
1 tsp ground cumin

Freshly ground black pepper
4 cups [960 ml] Basic Chicken Stock
    (page 29)
Avocado Crema (page 164) for topping
Quick Pickled Radishes (page 171)
    for topping

|||||||||||||||||||||||||||||||

1. In a large bowl, combine the beans and enough cold water to cover, and let soak, covered, overnight. Drain the beans, rinse under cold running water, and drain again.

2. Transfer the beans to a large stockpot and add enough cold water to cover by 3 in [7.5 cm]. Add the bay leaf, quartered onion, peppercorns, thyme, and parsley; season with salt; and bring to a boil over high heat. Turn the heat to low, cover, and cook for 1 hour. The beans will be tender but not totally cooked through. Drain the beans, discarding the cooking water and aromatics. Transfer the beans to a bowl and reserve. Clean out the stockpot.

3. In the cleaned stockpot over low heat, warm the olive oil. Add the chorizo and cook for 5 minutes. Add the chopped onions, garlic, and cumin; season with salt and pepper; and cook, stirring frequently, for 10 minutes. Turn the heat to high, add the chicken stock and 2 cups [480 ml] water, and bring to a boil. Turn the heat to low, add the reserved beans, and simmer, covered, for 1½ to 2 hours, or until the beans are almost falling apart, soft enough to thicken the soup. Taste and adjust the seasoning, adding more salt and pepper if needed.

4. Ladle the soup into mugs or bowls, top each with a spoonful of avocado crema and a few slices of pickled radish, and serve.

TO GO: Pack the avocado crema and the pickled radishes separately.

SICILIAN BLACK LENTIL SOUP
WITH GUANCIALE AND GRATED ORANGE

MAKES 10 TO 12 TASTING PORTIONS OR 8 FULL SERVINGS

Sicily is famous for its tiny black lentils, *lenticchie nere*. If you can't find Italian black lentils, look for black Beluga lentils (said to resemble caviar) or European brown lentils. There's no soaking involved with lentils, which means that this soup comes together in a little over an hour.

Guanciale is Italian cured pork jowl or cheek. The word *guancia* is Italian for "cheek." (For a vegetarian version of this soup, omit the *guanciale* and use vegetable broth.) Pancetta is Italian bacon from pork belly that is cured with salt, black pepper, and spices. Serve with Red Cabbage Salad with Blue Cheese and Maple-Glazed Walnuts (page 158).

2 large leeks
2½ Tbsp olive oil
2¾ oz [75 g] *guanciale* or pancetta, chopped into small cubes
1½ Tbsp chopped fresh rosemary
2 medium carrots, peeled and diced
1½ cups [340 g] Sicilian black lentils or European brown lentils, washed and picked over
1 Tbsp tomato paste
1 cup [240 ml] dry Italian white or red wine

8 cups [2 L] Basic Chicken Stock (page 29), Rich Beef-Bone Broth (page 24), or Vegetable Stock (page 34)
⅓ cup [20 g] chopped fresh parsley
Sea salt
Freshly ground black pepper
1½ tsp freshly grated orange or tangerine zest
Orange-flavored olive oil for drizzling (optional)

||||||||||||||||||||||||||||||

1. Trim off the dark green sections from the leeks and save for making vegetable stock. Halve the pale green and white sections lengthwise. Rinse under cold running water, pat dry, and cut crosswise into ½-in [12-mm] pieces.

2. In a large stockpot over low heat, warm the olive oil. (If your *guanciale* is particularly fatty, cut the amount of olive oil in half.) Add the *guanciale* and cook, stirring frequently, for 2 minutes.

3. Add the leeks to the pot and cook, stirring occasionally, for 6 minutes. Add the rosemary and carrots and cook for another 5 minutes. Stir in the lentils

and tomato paste and continue stirring to make sure that everything is evenly coated with the tomato paste. Turn the heat to high, add the wine, and bring to a boil. Cook for 1 minute. Add the chicken stock and turn the heat to low. Add half of the parsley, season with salt and pepper, and simmer, covered, for 45 minutes to 1 hour, or until the lentils are cooked (they should be al dente, not super-soft or falling apart). Taste and adjust the seasoning, adding more salt and pepper if needed.

4. Ladle the soup into mugs or bowls, top each with a generous sprinkling of orange zest and a sprinkling of the remaining parsley. Drizzle with orange-flavored olive oil, if desired, and serve.

TO GO: Pack the parsley and orange zest (and orange-flavored olive oil) in separate containers and add just before serving.

LAMB AND LENTIL SOUP
WITH LAMB MEATBALLS

MAKES 10 TO 12 TASTING PORTIONS OR 8 FULL PORTIONS

Leg of lamb roasted with lots of rosemary and garlic is one of my favorite meals. We eat leftovers for several nights, and then comes the payoff: the lamb bone can be used to make stock and then this soup. Lamb stock is strangely rich and subtle all at the same time and makes a delicious base for soup. The stock is combined with sautéed leeks, carrots, tomatoes, lentils, and delicious ground lamb-rosemary meatballs. Serve with warm crusty bread and Mixed Greens Salad with Mint-Tangerine Vinaigrette (page 156).

SOUP
1 large leek
1½ Tbsp olive oil
1 large garlic clove, chopped
1½ Tbsp chopped fresh rosemary
1½ Tbsp chopped fresh thyme
Sea salt
Freshly ground black pepper
2 medium carrots, peeled and cut crosswise into ½-in [12-mm] pieces
1 cup [220 g] brown lentils, washed and picked over
1 cup [240 g] canned crushed tomatoes with their juice
6 cups [1.4 L] "Recycled" Lamb Stock (page 28) or Roasted Chicken Stock (page 30)
½ cup [30 g] packed chopped fresh parsley

LAMB MEATBALLS
12 oz [340 g] ground lamb
1 garlic clove, finely chopped
1½ Tbsp chopped fresh rosemary
1 Tbsp chopped fresh thyme
1 egg
½ cup [40 g] freshly grated Parmesan or Romano cheese
½ cup [40 g] panko (Japanese bread crumbs)
Sea salt
Freshly ground black pepper
1 Tbsp olive oil
1½ tsp canola oil

GARNISHES
½ cup [30 g] packed finely chopped fresh parsley
½ cup [40 g] freshly grated Parmesan cheese

1. **TO MAKE THE SOUP:** Trim off the dark green section from the leek and save for making vegetable stock. Halve the pale green and white section lengthwise. Rinse under cold running water, pat dry, and cut crosswise into thin pieces.

2. In a large stockpot over low heat, warm the olive oil. Add the leek and garlic to the pot and cook, stirring, for 5 minutes. Add half of the rosemary and half of the thyme, season with salt and pepper, and cook for 1 minute. Add the carrots and cook, stirring, for 2 minutes. Add the lentils and tomatoes and stir to coat all the ingredients with the tomatoes. Turn the heat to high, add the lamb stock, and bring to a boil. Turn the heat to low; add the remaining rosemary, remaining thyme, and the parsley; and simmer, partially covered, for 45 minutes.

3. **TO MAKE THE MEATBALLS:** Meanwhile, in a medium bowl, combine the ground lamb, garlic, rosemary, thyme, egg, cheese, panko, and a generous sprinkling of salt and pepper. Using your hands, mix the ingredients thoroughly. Divide the mixture into about 30 small meatballs.

4. In a large skillet over medium-high heat, warm the olive oil with the canola oil. Working in batches to avoid crowding the skillet, cook the meatballs, rolling them around In the hot skillet, for about 5 minutes, or until evenly browned. Using a slotted spoon, transfer them to paper towels to drain. Repeat with the remaining meatballs. The goal is to brown them on the outside without cooking them all the way through; they will finish cooking in the soup.

5. When the soup has finished simmering, add the meatballs. Once all the meatballs are in the soup, cover the pot, and continue cooking for another 30 to 45 minutes, or until the lentils and carrots are tender and the meatballs are cooked through. Taste and adjust the seasoning, adding more salt and pepper if needed. If the soup tastes weak, remove the cover and simmer over medium heat for another 10 minutes.

6. Ladle the soup into mugs or bowls, sprinkle with either or both of the garnishes, and serve.

TO GO: Pack the parsley and the grated cheese separately. Once you add the meatballs, simmer the soup for 25 to 30 minutes and then remove from the heat. Reheat the soup at the party to finish cooking the meatballs.

LAMB AND FARRO SOUP
WITH SPRING VEGETABLES

MAKES 16 TO 18 TASTING PORTIONS OR 10 TO 12 FULL SERVINGS

DF

Farro is a whole grain with a great, nutty texture. Here, it is simmered in a lamb stock with pieces of lamb, spring vegetables, fresh dill, and parsley. Despite its delicate flavor, this soup somehow also feels hearty. Try to make it a day ahead or give it several hours to chill to remove any excess fat that forms on top. Serve with Buttery Biscuits (page 155).

⅓ cup [30 g] all-purpose flour

Sea salt

Freshly ground black pepper

1½ lb [680 g] lamb shoulder, cut into 1-in [2.5-cm] pieces

2 Tbsp olive oil

1½ Tbsp canola oil

2 medium leeks

3 garlic cloves, finely chopped

2 celery stalks, cut crosswise into ½-in [12-mm] pieces

4 medium carrots, peeled and cut crosswise into ½-in [12-mm] pieces

3 medium parsnips, peeled and cut crosswise into ½-in [12-mm] pieces

1 Tbsp tomato paste

4 Tbsp [15 g] packed minced fresh chives

⅔ cup [40 g] packed finely chopped fresh parsley

⅔ cup [40 g] packed finely chopped fresh dill

1 cup [220 g] farro

⅔ cup [160 ml] dry white wine

12 cups [2.8 L] "Recycled" Lamb Stock (page 28), Basic Chicken Stock (page 29), or Roasted Chicken Stock (page 30)

1. In a medium bowl, season the flour with salt and pepper. Dredge the lamb pieces lightly in the seasoned flour, shaking off any excess.

2. In a large stockpot over medium-high heat, warm 1 Tbsp of the olive oil and all of the canola oil. Working in batches and without crowding the pot, brown the lamb pieces, stirring occasionally, for about 5 minutes per batch, or until golden brown. Using a slotted spoon, transfer the meat to paper towels to drain. Using a paper towel, remove the oil from the pot.

3. Trim off the dark green sections from the leeks and save for making vegetable stock. Halve the pale green and white sections lengthwise. Rinse under cold running water, pat dry, and cut crosswise into thin pieces.

continued

4. In the cleaned stockpot over low heat, warm the remaining 1 Tbsp olive oil. Add the leeks and cook, stirring, for 8 minutes. Add the garlic and cook for 2 minutes. Add the celery, carrots, and parsnips; season with salt and pepper; and cook, stirring, for 5 minutes. Add the tomato paste and stir to evenly coat the vegetables. Stir in 2 Tbsp of the chives, ⅓ cup [20 g] of the parsley, ⅓ cup [20 g] of the dill, and the farro. Turn the heat to high, add the wine, and bring to a boil. Then add the lamb stock and bring back to a boil. Turn the heat to low, partially cover, and simmer for 45 minutes to 1 hour, or until the farro is cooked but not overly soft (it should still have an al dente bite) and the lamb is tender. Taste and adjust the seasoning, adding more salt and pepper if needed.

5. Ladle the soup into mugs or bowls, and serve with a sprinkling of the remaining chives, parsley, and dill.

TO GO: Simmer the soup for only 45 minutes. Reheat at the party until the farro and lamb are tender. Pack the chive, parsley, and dill garnishes separately.

ITALIAN WEDDING SOUP

MAKES 15 TO 20 TASTING PORTIONS OR 10 TO 12 FULL SERVINGS

There are conflicting stories about how this soup got its name. Here's what I know: It's Italian and generally made with chicken stock, vegetables, small meatballs, Swiss chard or escarole, and tiny pasta. What most of the stories have in common is that the ingredients are said to "marry," or come together, in a beautiful, loving soup. Although the method for making the meatballs is listed first, you can easily accomplish the task while the soup is simmering. Often eggs and cheese are stirred into the stock at the end, like an Italian egg-drop soup, but I like to keep the soup a bit more straightforward. Serve with Herbed Ricotta Toasts with Slow-Roasted Cherry Tomatoes (page 152).

MEATBALLS
8 oz [230 g] ground beef
8 oz [230 g] ground pork or veal
1 egg, lightly beaten
½ cup [40 g] freshly grated Parmesan cheese
½ cup [40 g] bread crumbs or panko (Japanese bread crumbs)
2 garlic cloves, very finely chopped
3 Tbsp very thinly sliced fresh basil

¼ cup [15 g] packed finely chopped fresh parsley
Sea salt
Freshly ground black pepper
1½ Tbsp olive oil

SOUP
2 Tbsp olive oil
1 medium onion, finely chopped
2 shallots, finely chopped
3 garlic cloves, very thinly sliced
Sea salt
Freshly ground black pepper
4 medium carrots, peeled and cut crosswise into ½-in [12-mm] pieces
4 large celery stalks with leaves, thinly sliced
2 cups [480 g] canned diced or crushed tomatoes with their juice
⅓ cup [20 g] packed very thinly sliced fresh basil
¼ cup [15 g] packed finely chopped fresh parsley
12 cups [2.8 L] Basic Chicken Stock (page 29) or Roasted Chicken Stock (page 30)
½ cup [50 g] orzo or other small pasta shape, like stars or *tubetini*
1 lb [455 g] Swiss chard or escarole with stems, cut into thin ribbonlike shreds

GARNISHES
½ cup [40 g] freshly grated Parmesan cheese
¼ cup [15 g] packed very thinly sliced fresh basil
½ cup [30 g] packed finely chopped fresh parsley

IIIIIIIIIIIIIIIIIIIIIIIIIIIII

1. **TO MAKE THE MEATBALLS:** In a large bowl, combine the ground beef, ground pork, egg, Parmesan, bread crumbs, garlic, basil, and parsley and season with salt and pepper. Using your hands, mix well, making sure that all the ingredients are evenly incorporated. Divide the mixture into 30 small meatballs.

2. In a large skillet over medium-high heat, warm the olive oil. Working in batches to avoid crowding the skillet, cook the meatballs, rolling them around in the hot skillet, for about 3 minutes, or until evenly browned. Using a slotted spoon, transfer them to paper towels to drain. Repeat with the remaining meatballs. Set aside.

continued

3. **TO MAKE THE SOUP:** In a large stockpot over low heat, warm the olive oil. Add the onion, shallots, and garlic; season with salt and pepper; and cook for 10 minutes. Add the carrots and celery and cook for 5 minutes. Add the tomatoes, basil, and parsley and cook for another 2 minutes. Turn the heat to high, add the chicken stock, and bring to a boil. Turn the heat to low, cover, and simmer gently for 45 minutes.

4. When the soup has finished simmering, remove the lid and add the meatballs. Turn the heat to medium and heat the soup until it begins to simmer. Then, turn the heat to medium-low, add the pasta and Swiss chard, and simmer, covered, for 10 to 12 minutes, or until the pasta is almost tender, or al dente, and the meatballs are cooked through. Taste and adjust the seasoning, adding more salt and pepper if needed.

5. Ladle the soup into mugs or bowls, sprinkle with any or all of the garnishes, and serve.

TO GO: *After adding the meatballs to the soup, take the soup off the heat. Add the pasta and Swiss chard but do not return the soup to the heat. At the party, reheat the soup and simmer until the pasta is almost tender and the meatballs are cooked through. Pack the garnishes in separate containers.*

BEEF-BARLEY MUSHROOM SOUP

MAKES 10 TO 12 TASTING PORTIONS OR 6 TO 8 FULL SERVINGS

This rich, hearty version of beef-barley soup features cubes of beef chuck, dried and fresh mushrooms, and barley. The recipe comes from friend Stephanie Guay Deihl, writer and mom of three who blogs about family-style cooking at OneFamilyMeal.com. Serve with Buttery Biscuits (page 155).

½ oz [15 g] dried porcini mushrooms
1½ lb [680 g] beef chuck, cut into 2-in [5-cm] chunks
Sea salt
Freshly ground black pepper
2 Tbsp olive oil
1 large leek
2 Tbsp unsalted butter
1 large onion, diced
2 large carrots, peeled and diced
1 cup [240 ml] red wine
4 cups [960 ml] Basic Beef Stock (page 27), Rich Beef-Bone Broth (page 24), or Basic Chicken Stock (page 29)
10 oz [280 g] cremini (also called baby bella) mushrooms, stemmed, cleaned, and quartered
3 Tbsp coarsely chopped fresh thyme
1½ Tbsp coarsely chopped fresh rosemary
½ cup [110 g] pearled barley
1 to 2 tsp red wine vinegar
1 cup [80 g] freshly grated Parmesan cheese

||||||||||||||||||||||||||||||||||

1. In a small bowl, combine the porcini mushrooms and 1 cup [240 ml] boiling water and let soak for 10 minutes.

2. Meanwhile, season the beef with salt and pepper. In a wide, deep 5- to 6-qt [4.7- to 5.7-L] stockpot or Dutch oven over medium heat, warm the olive oil. Working in batches to avoid crowding the pan (the pieces should fit in a single layer without overlapping), sear the beef for 2 to 3 minutes per side, until it begins to brown. Do not cook through. Using a slotted spoon, transfer the beef to a medium bowl as it is browned. Pour off all but 1 Tbsp of the fat from the pot; set aside.

3. Trim off the dark green section from the leek and save for making vegetable stock. Halve the pale green and white section lengthwise. Rinse under cold running water, pat dry, and cut crosswise into thin pieces.

4. Add the butter to the oil in the stockpot and set over low heat. Add the leek, onion, and carrots and cook for about 5 minutes, until the vegetables are slightly tender. Turn the heat to medium-high, add the wine, and cook for 2 minutes, until the alcohol scent wears off, scraping up the browned bits clinging to the bottom of the pot.

5. Remove the porcini mushrooms from the bowl, reserving the soaking liquid, and coarsely chop the mushrooms. Strain the liquid through cheesecloth into a bowl; reserve.

6. Add the beef stock, reserved soaking liquid, porcini, cremini, thyme, rosemary, and seared beef to the pot; season with salt and pepper; and stir to combine. Turn the heat to high and bring the mixture to a boil. Turn the heat to low and simmer, partially covered, for 20 minutes. Stir in the barley, cover, and simmer for another 45 minutes, or until the barley is almost tender, or al dente. Remove from the heat, add 1 tsp of the vinegar, and stir to combine. Taste and adjust the seasoning adding more vinegar, salt, and pepper if needed.

7. Ladle the soup into mugs or bowls and serve, passing the Parmesan on the side.

TO GO: Pack the grated cheese separately.

RUSSIAN-STYLE BEEF BORSCHT

MAKES 10 TO 12 TASTING PORTIONS OR 6 TO 8 FULL SERVINGS

This is the soup for those bitter cold winter days when you think nothing can possibly warm you up. Hearty, rich, and full of sweet, earthy beets, carrots, onions, leeks, and beef broth, this borscht should be served in small bowls with a dollop of sour cream, a sprinkling of chopped fresh dill, and a pinch of cracked pepper.

I like to make this soup after I've made Rich Beef-Bone Broth or after I've roasted a beef brisket, short ribs, or even roast beef. The leftover meat is delicious added to the soup. Serve with Mixed Greens Salad with Mint-Tangerine Vinaigrette (page 156).

2 medium leeks

2 Tbsp butter

1 Tbsp olive oil

1 lb [455 g] beets, peeled and finely chopped

4 medium carrots, peeled and finely chopped

1 small onion, finely chopped

1 small head white cabbage, very thinly shredded or thinly sliced

3 Tbsp finely chopped fresh dill, plus 1 cup [55 g] packed finely chopped fresh dill

1 Tbsp finely chopped fresh thyme

Sea salt

Coarsely ground black pepper

1½ Tbsp juniper berries (optional)

2 Tbsp coriander seeds (optional)

3 cups [720 g] canned chopped tomatoes with their juice

1 cup [240 ml] dry red wine

2 cups [480 ml] Rich Beef-Bone Broth (page 24), Basic Beef Stock (page 27), or canned low-sodium broth

2 cups [480 ml] water

3 Tbsp red wine vinegar

2 cups [320 g] finely chopped cooked beef from a brisket, short ribs, or roast beef (optional)

1 cup [190 g] sour cream or plain Greek yogurt

1. Trim off the dark green sections from the leeks and save for making vegetable stock. Halve the pale green and white sections lengthwise. Rinse under cold running water, pat dry, and cut crosswise into small pieces.

2. In a large stockpot over low heat, warm the butter and olive oil. Add the leeks, beets, carrots, onion, cabbage, 3 Tbsp dill, and thyme; season with salt and pepper; and stir well. Cover and cook for 10 minutes.

continued

3. Meanwhile, if desired, cut out a 2-in [5-cm] piece of cheesecloth. Wrap up the juniper berries and coriander seeds and tie with a piece of kitchen string. Add the herb bundle to the pot and cover it with the vegetables.

4. Add the tomatoes, wine, beef broth, and water to the pot and bring to a boil over high heat. Turn the heat to low, cover, and simmer for about 45 minutes. Add the vinegar and cooked beef (if using). Taste and adjust the seasoning, adding more salt and pepper if needed. Simmer for another 10 minutes. The vegetables should be tender, and the stock should be very flavorful; the soup will be quite thick. Remove the cheesecloth with the spices.

5. Ladle the soup into mugs or bowls; garnish with a dollop of sour cream, a sprinkling of the remaining dill, and a pinch of pepper; and serve.

TO GO: Pack the garnishes separately.

SHORT-RIB RAMEN
WITH SOY EGGS

MAKES 12 TASTING PORTIONS OR 8 FULL SERVINGS

Making rich beef-bone broth *is* a time commitment but a worthwhile one. You wind up with a pot of beautiful rich stock as well as the base for this ramen because both the broth and the meat are used. Make the broth at least a day ahead in order to chill and remove the fat properly. The soy eggs also need to marinate for several hours, so plan your time accordingly. But once the broth, meat, and soy eggs have been prepared, the ramen comes together pretty quickly and easily.

SOY EGGS

2 Tbsp mirin (rice wine)

¼ cup [60 ml] sake

¾ cup [180 ml] soy sauce or tamari

1 Tbsp sugar

4 to 6 eggs

RAMEN

8 cups [2 L] Rich Beef-Bone Broth (page 24), Basic Beef Stock (page 27), or canned low-sodium broth

1 Tbsp very thinly sliced fresh peeled ginger

2 Tbsp finely chopped fresh cilantro

8 oz [230 g] ramen, somen, or Udon noodles

12 oz [340 g] firm tofu, cut into ½-in [12-mm] cubes

4 scallions, cut crosswise into 1-in [2.5-cm] pieces

12 oz [340 g] cooked short rib, meat from shank from beef-bone broth, or leftover beef from brisket or roast beef, shredded or cut into ½- to 1-in [12-mm to 2.5-cm] pieces

4 oz [120 g] fresh sugar snap peas, very thinly sliced

4 oz [120 g] watercress or pea tendrils

GARNISHES

½ cup [20 g] packed chopped fresh cilantro

4 scallions, very thinly sliced

Soy sauce or tamari for serving (optional)

1. **TO MAKE THE SOY EGGS:** In a medium stockpot, combine the mirin, sake, soy sauce, and sugar with 3 cups [720 ml] cold water and bring to a boil over high heat. Turn the heat to low and simmer for 8 minutes. Remove from the heat and let cool. Transfer to a large mason jar.

2. Place the eggs in a small saucepan, add enough cold water to cover, and bring to a boil over high heat. Turn the heat to low and cook for 5 minutes for small eggs or 6 minutes for larger ones. Remove from the heat, drain, and rinse under cold running water. When the eggs are cool enough to handle, crack the shells and peel them. Place the peeled eggs in the soy mixture and let marinate for about 1 hour.

continued

3. **TO MAKE THE RAMEN:** In a large stockpot over medium heat, combine the beef broth, ginger, and cilantro and bring to a simmer. Continue to simmer for about 10 minutes.

4. Meanwhile, bring another large stockpot of lightly salted water to a boil over high heat. Add the noodles and cook for 3 to 5 minutes, depending on the type of noodle you're using, until almost tender. Drain and divide the cooked noodles equally among mugs or bowls, making sure to separate the noodles so they don't clump.

5. Add the tofu, scallions, and cooked beef to the simmering broth and simmer for 4 minutes, until heated through. Just before serving, add the peas and watercress. You want just to wilt the peas and watercress, not fully cook them.

6. Remove the eggs from the marinade and halve lengthwise.

7. Divide the broth, vegetables, and meat equally among the soup bowls containing the cooked noodles. Top each serving with one-half of a soy egg and sprinkle with the cilantro and scallions. Serve with soy sauce on the side, if desired.

TO GO: The soup can be prepared without adding the peas and watercress, both of which should be packed separately. Pack the prepared eggs separately. Pack the noodles with 2 to 3 Tbsp water or broth (to keep them from clumping) in a covered container. Reheat the soup at the party, drain the noodles and add with the peas, noodles, and watercress at the last minute, and serve as directed.

PORK AND WHITE BEAN CHILI

MAKES 8 TO 10 TASTING PORTIONS OR 6 FULL SERVINGS

This chili involves several steps, a few of which are a bit time intensive, so it's a good idea to make it a day or two ahead of your party. The meat needs to marinate for at least six hours, and if you opt to make your own beans instead of using canned beans, you will need extra time.

This chili goes well with all kinds of tasty accompaniments, including but not limited to slices of avocado, lime wedges, sour cream, chopped fresh cilantro, chopped scallions, and a variety of hot-pepper sauces. Party-goers will appreciate having tortilla chips or warm corn tortillas for sopping up the flavorful juices. Skillet Corn Bread with Chive and Brown Butter (page 154) would also pair very well.

1 tsp cumin seeds or ½ tsp ground cumin

2 lb [910 g] pork shoulder, excess fat removed, cut into 1- to 1½-in [2.5- to 4-cm] cubes

½ cup [120 ml] dry red wine

6 dried whole de árbol chiles, New Mexican chiles, or red chiles

2 garlic cloves, chopped

1 small onion, chopped

1 Tbsp canned chipotle chile in adobo sauce

1 tsp dried oregano

Sea salt

Freshly ground black pepper

1 Tbsp canola oil

One 28-oz [750-g] can diced or chopped tomatoes with their juice

3 cups [660 g] cooked white cannellini beans (see page 107) or canned beans (drained, rinsed, and re-drained)

⅓ cup [20 g] packed chopped fresh cilantro

½ to 1 tsp chili powder (depending on how spicy you like your chili)

One 12-oz [355-ml] bottle of beer, preferably dark

GARNISHES

1 lime, cut into 8 to 10 small wedges

Avocado slices or chunks

½ cup [30 g] packed chopped fresh cilantro

4 scallions, finely chopped

1 cup [190 g] sour cream

Hot-pepper sauce

Tortilla chips or warm corn tortillas

1. In an ungreased skillet over low heat, toast the cumin seeds for about 6 minutes, or until fragrant. Remove from the heat and grind in a spice grinder or in a coffee grinder used exclusively for spices, or grind with a mortar and pestle. Set aside.

2. Place the pork in a large bowl, add the wine, and set aside.

3. Place the dried chiles in a small bowl, add 1 cup [240 ml] boiling water, and let soak for 15 minutes. Remove the softened chiles from the bowl. Strain the soaking liquid and reserve.

4. In a blender, combine the toasted cumin, garlic, onion, rehydrated chiles, 1 cup [240 ml] reserved soaking liquid, chipotle chile, and oregano; season with salt and pepper; and process until thick and blended. The marinade will be chunky; it doesn't need to be perfectly smooth.

5. Pour the marinade over the pork. Using your hands, mix the meat with the marinade until the meat is thoroughly coated. Cover and refrigerate for at least 6 hours, or up to overnight.

6. Using a slotted spoon, transfer the pork to a medium bowl, reserving the marinade.

7. In a large stockpot over high heat, warm the canola oil until it is hot. Working in batches to avoid crowding the pot, cook the pork for about 2 minutes per side, or until browned. Using a slotted spoon, transfer the pork to paper towels to drain. (You shouldn't need to add more oil to the pot since the pork will render some fat.)

8. Add the tomatoes to the pot and stir, using the side of the spoon to break them into smaller pieces. Add ½ cup [120 ml] water and bring to a boil over high heat. Turn the heat to low; add the beans, cilantro, chili powder, reserved marinade, and beer; and season with salt and pepper. Cover and simmer for about 1 hour. Turn the heat to very low and simmer gently, partially covered, for another 30 minutes, or until the meat is tender and the sauce is flavorful and somewhat reduced. Taste and adjust the seasoning, adding more salt and pepper if needed.

9. Ladle the chili into mugs or bowls and serve with any or all of the garnishes.

TO GO: Pack the garnishes separately. Reheat the chili at the party and serve the garnishes on the side.

FISH & SEAFOOD SOUPS & CHOWDERS

Living in Maine means having access to great seafood and shellfish. There's our world-famous lobster, of course, but we also have fabulous clams, mussels, and oysters. And New England chefs use these gifts from the sea to make delicious chowders, stews, and soups. But, in addition to East Coast–inspired soups, I've had fun experimenting with soups from the West Coast; the popular cioppino as well as Tomales Bay oyster stew and Chorizo and Clam Stew. I went even farther afield by including a French bouillabaisse-like fish soup and a rich Scottish smoked haddock and leek chowder. Some of these more sophisticated fish soups are complicated to travel with, so you might want to consider making them on a night when you're hosting a soup swap at home.

CIOPPINO

MAKES 10 TO 12 TASTING PORTIONS OR 8 FULL PORTIONS

Cioppino appears on menus all over the Bay Area. Originally from the Ligurian word *ciuppin*, meaning "chopped," the soup was said to have been created by fishermen from Genoa, Italy, who settled in Northern California, chopping up any bits and pieces of fish that were left over at the end of a long day fishing. This is my version, a hearty tomato-based soup full of sweet Dungeness crab, cod, shrimp, clams, and mussels. Serve it with warm sourdough or Buttery Biscuits (page 155). Mixed Greens Salad with Mint-Tangerine Vinaigrette (page 156) would be a great accompaniment to this rich soup.

NOTE: If you don't have access to Dungeness crab, you can substitute lobster. Very carefully remove the rubber bands from the claws (the lobsters can pinch, so pay attention). Place two ½-lb lobsters shell-side down in 1½ in [4 cm] of lightly salted boiling water and steam for about 10 minutes, until it is almost cooked, and set aside to cool. Remove the meat from the shell and cut into big chunks. You can also substitute East Coast crab, but it's not quite the same.

2 medium leeks

2 Tbsp olive oil

4 garlic cloves, chopped

2 medium onions, chopped

1 large red or yellow bell pepper, cored and chopped into ½-in [12-mm] pieces

⅓ cup [20 g] packed julienned fresh basil

2 Tbsp chopped fresh thyme

1½ Tbsp tomato paste

Sea salt

Freshly ground black pepper

Two 28-oz [794-g] cans crushed tomatoes with basil

4 cups [960 ml] Fish Stock (page 33)

1¼ cups [300 ml] dry white wine

4 lb [1.8 kg] Dungeness crabs, cleaned, cooked, cracked, and quartered or cut into smaller pieces if very large

1 lb [455 g] black cod or regular cod, cut into 2-in [5-cm] pieces

8 oz [230 g] large shell-on shrimp, deveined

1½ lb [680 g] littleneck clams, scrubbed clean

1 lb [455 g] mussels, scrubbed clean, debearded, and any cracked shells discarded

8 Croutes (page 167) or thick slices of toasted crusty bread

1. Trim off the dark green sections from the leeks and save for making vegetable stock. Halve the pale green and white sections lengthwise. Rinse under cold running water, pat dry, and cut crosswise into thin pieces.

2. In a large stockpot over low heat, warm the olive oil. Add the leeks, garlic, and onions and cook, stirring, for 10 minutes. Add the bell pepper and cook for 5 minutes. Add half of the basil, the thyme, tomato paste, a pinch of salt, and a pinch of pepper and cook, stirring to coat the vegetables with the paste, for 2 minutes. Turn the heat to high; add the crushed tomatoes, fish stock, and wine; and bring to a boil. After about 2 minutes, turn the heat to low, partially cover, and cook for 20 minutes.

3. Add the crabs to the pot and cook for 5 minutes. Add the cod and cook for 2 minutes. Add the shrimp and clams and cook for another 4 minutes. Add the mussels and cook until the shellfish are just open. Taste and adjust the seasoning, adding more salt and pepper if needed. Add the remaining basil. Discard any shellfish that don't open.

4. Ladle the cioppino into mugs or bowls, top each with a croute, and serve.

TO GO: Add the crab and cod to the hot soup, cover, and remove from the heat. Pack the remaining fish (shrimp, clams, and mussels) separately. Pack the croutes and the remaining basil in separate containers. At the party, bring the soup to a simmer over low heat; add the shrimp, clams, and mussels; and cook until the shellfish open.

PROVENÇAL-STYLE FISH SOUP WITH ROUILLE

MAKES 12 TO 14 TASTING PORTIONS OR 8 TO 10 FULL SERVINGS

This is my take on bouillabaisse. The soup, which is made with a flavor-rich combination of leeks, tomatoes, fennel, carrot, and celery, provides the base for the briny clams, mussels, lobster, scallops, shrimp, and firm white fish. Making this soup involves several steps, but it is a feast, a main-course Saturday-night-showstopper of a soup. But it can be adapted for a soup supper by doing some prep work and following a few easy steps. Serve with rouille and crusty bread for soaking up all the tasty broth. Get ready for an onslaught of compliments.

2 medium leeks

2 Tbsp olive oil

2 large celery stalks, finely chopped

1 small carrot, peeled and finely chopped

1 small fennel bulb, cored and finely chopped

4 garlic cloves, thinly sliced

1 Tbsp finely chopped fresh thyme or 1 tsp dried, crumbled

½ tsp crumbled saffron threads

¼ cup [15 g] packed finely chopped fresh parsley

8 oz [230 g] medium shell-on shrimp

¾ cup [180 ml] dry white wine

2 cups [480 g] canned crushed tomatoes with their juice

6 cups [1.4 L] Fish Stock (page 33)

Sea salt

Freshly ground black pepper

One 1½-lb [680-g] live lobster

1 lb [455 g] cod, haddock, or any firm white fish, cut into 1-in [2.5-cm] pieces

6½ oz [185 g] sea scallops

2½ lb [1.2 kg] littleneck clams, scrubbed clean

2 lb [910 g] mussels, scrubbed clean, debearded, and any cracked shells discarded

Crusty bread or Croutes (page 167) for serving

Rouille (page 167) for serving

1. Trim off the dark green sections from the leeks and save for making vegetable stock. Halve the pale green and white sections lengthwise. Rinse under cold running water, pat dry, and cut crosswise into thin pieces.

2. In a large stockpot over low heat, warm the olive oil. Add the leeks and cook, stirring, for 6 minutes. Stir in the celery, carrot, fennel, half of the garlic, the thyme, half of the saffron, and the parsley and cook for another 6 minutes.

3. Meanwhile, peel the shrimp, leaving the tails attached and reserving the shells. Devein the shrimp by cutting a shallow slit in the back so you can remove the thin black intestine. Set the shrimp aside covered in plastic in the refrigerator.

continued

4. Cut a large square of cheesecloth, place the shrimp shells in the middle, and tie the ends of the cloth together to form a bundle.

5. Turn the heat under the pot to high and add the wine, tomatoes, fish stock, a pinch of salt, and a generous grinding of pepper. Add the cheesecloth bundle, making sure it is totally submerged in the liquid, and bring to a boil. Turn the heat to low and cook, partially covered, for 30 minutes. Taste and adjust the seasoning, adding more salt and pepper if needed. Remove the pot from the heat and let cool slightly.

6. Using a slotted spoon, remove the cheesecloth bundle and, holding it over the pot, squeeze with the back of another spoon to release all the juice. (At this point, you can cover and refrigerate the soup base for up to 1 day.)

7. Bring the soup base to a simmer over medium-high heat. Very carefully remove the rubber bands from the lobster claws (the lobster can pinch you, so pay attention). Place the lobster, shell-side down, in the pot, cover, and cook for 8 minutes. You may need to spoon some of the soup over the lobster a few times to keep it submerged.

8. Meanwhile, season the cod and the scallops with the remaining saffron and a pinch of salt and pepper. Set aside.

9. Using tongs, remove the lobster, letting any bits from the soup drain back into the pot, and let cool. When the lobster is cool (it will *not* be fully cooked), remove the meat from the claws and tail and cut into 1-in [2.5-cm] pieces; reserve. The body can be saved for snacking, or you can cut it up into four pieces to add to the soup for a very rustic look. Add the cod and lobster meat to the pot and cook for 3 minutes. Add the clams and mussels. When the shellfish just start to open, add the shrimp and scallops and cook until all the shellfish is open and the fish is tender and cooked through. Discard any shellfish that don't open.

10. Ladle the soup into mugs or bowls and serve with crusty bread. Pass the rouille so that guests can spread as much as they like on their bread.

TO GO: To be honest, this is a tough soup to travel with. I always make it when people are coming to my house. However, it can be done. Make the soup base, let cool slightly, and cook the lobster. Remove the lobster meat from the shell and cut it into pieces as instructed. Add the cod and lobster pieces to the soup. At the party, reheat the soup and add the clams, mussels, shrimp, and scallops and cook over medium-low heat until the shellfish open and the fish is tender. Pack the rouille and crusty bread separately.

TOMALES BAY OYSTER STEW

MAKES 10 TO 12 TASTING PORTIONS OR 6 TO 8 FULL SERVINGS

I was visiting my daughter, Emma, in San Francisco, and she asked if I was "up for a food adventure?" That's like asking an artist if she'd like to visit the Louvre. Off we went to Tomales Bay, near the famed Point Reyes National Seashore in Northern California. The Tomales Bay Oyster Company is a no-frills kind of place nestled on the shore where visitors pick out a picnic table with an adjoining barbecue (and view of the bay) and then buy freshly harvested oysters and clams. Emma brought everything else we would possibly need, including a stockpot and enough vegetables to make a soup or two—in my mind, a perfect way to spend the day.

A tribute to the briny bivalves, this simple oyster stew has very few ingredients. Because it's quite rich, I suggest using very small bowls and serving it with Citrus Salad with Crème Fraîche and Tarragon (page 159).

¾ cup [180 ml] heavy cream
1½ cups [360 ml] whole milk
6 Tbsp [85 g] butter
½ cup [90 g] finely chopped shallots
24 oysters, shucked, with all their liquor (juice)
Dash of Worcestershire sauce
Dash of hot-pepper sauce
Freshly ground black pepper
Dash of sweet paprika (optional)

|||||||||||||||||||||||||||||||

1. In a medium nonreactive saucepan over low heat, warm the cream and milk.

2. In a medium stockpot over low heat, melt the butter. Add the shallots and cook for 5 minutes. Add the oysters (but not the liquor) and cook for 1 minute. Using a slotted spoon, transfer the shallots and oysters to a medium bowl and set aside. Add the warm cream and milk mixture to the pot and bring to a simmer. Add the oyster liquor, Worcestershire, hot-pepper sauce, and reserved oysters and shallots; season with pepper; and cook for 2 minutes, until the soup is very hot and the oysters are just cooked through.

3. Ladle the stew into mugs or bowls, sprinkle with the paprika, if desired, and serve.

TO GO: After adding the cream and milk, remove the pot from the heat. When the soup is mostly cooled down and off the heat, add the oysters and shallots with the seasonings. At the party, reheat the soup over low heat for 2 to 3 minutes.

CHORIZO AND CLAM STEW
WITH TOMATOES AND ARUGULA

MAKES 10 TO 12 TASTING PORTIONS OR 8 FULL SERVINGS

This simple stew takes about 20 minutes from start to finish and makes a thoroughly satisfying meal. You sauté chorizo sausage with onions and shallots; add basil and parsley, fish stock, and white wine; and then throw in the clams. About 5 minutes later, once the clams have opened, you're ready to feast. Serve with Herbed Ricotta Toasts with Slow-Roasted Cherry Tomatoes (page 152) or Buttery Biscuits (page 155).

3 Tbsp olive oil

1 large onion, finely chopped

2 shallots, finely chopped

Sea salt

Freshly ground black pepper

10 oz [280 g] fresh chorizo, casing removed, or dried chorizo, thinly sliced or coarsely chopped

¼ cup [15 g] packed finely chopped fresh parsley

¼ cup [15 g] packed thinly sliced fresh basil

3 large ripe tomatoes (red, yellow, or heirloom variety), chopped

1½ cups [360 ml] dry white wine

6 cups [1.4 L] Fish Stock (page 33) or bottled clam juice

Dash of hot-pepper sauce

3 lb [1.4 kg] littleneck or Manila clams, scrubbed clean

4 cups [150 g] packed coarsely chopped baby arugula or arugula

1. In a large stockpot over low heat, warm the olive oil. Add the onion and shallots, a pinch each of salt and pepper and cook, stirring occasionally, for 8 minutes. Add the chorizo and cook, stirring and breaking up the sausage, for 5 minutes. Add the parsley, basil, and tomatoes and cook, stirring, for another 3 minutes. Turn the heat to high, add the wine, and bring to a boil for 1 minute. Add the fish stock and hot-pepper sauce and bring to a boil. Turn the heat to medium, cover, and cook for about 5 minutes. Add the clams and cook for 5 to 7 minutes, until they just begin to open. Discard any clams that don't open.

2. Using a slotted spoon, divide the clams equally among mugs or bowls. Ladle the soup over the clams, top with equal portions of arugula, and serve. The heat of the soup will just wilt the arugula.

TO GO: Make the soup without adding the clams or arugula. Pack them both separately. At the party, reheat the soup and then add the clams. Once they open, add the arugula and serve.

NEW ENGLAND FISH AND CLAM CHOWDER

MAKES 10 TO 12 TASTING PORTIONS OR 6 TO 8 FULL SERVINGS

There are endless variations of New England chowders, some that use only clams and others that rely on a wide variety of fish and shellfish. You can add lobster, mussels, or other firm fish, depending on where you live and what you have access to.

You can open your clams at home or you can ask your fishmonger to open them. If you opt for the latter, be sure to have him or her save all the clam juice. Don't open the clams more than a few hours ahead of time. You can also steam the clams over high heat with ¼ cup [60 ml] water until they just begin to open and then strain the juice so that no sand or grit goes into the chowder.

You'll need a total of 4 cups [960 ml] of dairy. But you can play with the proportions of milk—and whether you use low-fat or whole milk—and cream, depending on how rich you like your chowder. Chowder is traditionally served with oyster crackers, but you can also serve it with Buttery Biscuits.

6 strips country-style or thick-cut bacon or ½ cup [150 g] finely chopped salt pork (optional)

1 Tbsp olive oil, plus 1½ Tbsp if not using bacon

2 medium onions, finely chopped

Sea salt

Freshly ground black pepper

2 Tbsp chopped fresh thyme or 1½ tsp dried, crumbled

2 lb [910 g] potatoes, such as Yukon gold, peeled and cut into ½-in [12-mm] cubes

2 cups [480 ml] low-fat or whole milk

2 cups [480 ml] heavy cream

2 lb [910 g] haddock or other firm-flesh fish, cut into 1-in [2.5-cm] cubes

3 lb [1.4 kg] clams (cherrystone, littleneck, steamer, or Mahogany), opened raw and coarsely chopped, plus 1 cup [240 ml] clam juice (the juice is released when the clams are opened) or bottled clam juice or Fish Stock (page 33)

2 Tbsp all-purpose flour

1½ cups [360 ml] Fish Stock (page 33)

½ cup [30 g] packed finely chopped fresh parsley

Small pinch of cayenne pepper, plus more as needed

Buttery Biscuits (page 155) or Polenta Croutons (page 169) for serving (optional)

|||||||||||||||||||||||||||||||||||||

1. In a large stockpot over low heat, cook the bacon (if using) until crisp on both sides. Using tongs, transfer to paper towels to drain. Crumble the bacon into small pieces or, if you prefer, cut it into slightly larger pieces and set aside. Remove all but 1 Tbsp of fat from the pot.

2. Add the olive oil to the stockpot and warm over low heat. Add the onions and cook, stirring frequently, for about 6 minutes, or until the onions are soft and just beginning to turn color. Add just a pinch of salt (clams are very briny, i.e., salty) and pepper and half of the thyme, and stir well. Add the potatoes and cook, stirring, for about 1 minute, until the potatoes are thoroughly coated with the herbs and onions.

3. Meanwhile, in a medium nonreactive saucepan over medium heat, bring the milk and cream to a very gentle simmer.

4. Add the haddock and clams to the vegetables and stir for about 30 seconds. Add the flour. Cook, stirring the flour into the fish and vegetables, for about 1 minute. Turn the heat to medium-low. Add the clam juice and fish stock, stir well, and cook for about 2 minutes. Add half of the bacon and the remaining thyme and bring to a gentle simmer. Turn the heat to low and add half of the parsley and the cayenne. Cover and simmer gently for 10 minutes, or until the potatoes are tender.

5. Stir the warm milk mixture into the chowder. Taste and adjust the seasoning, adding more salt, pepper, and cayenne if needed, and cook another 3 to 4 minutes, or until the soup is quite hot.

6. Ladle the chowder into mugs or bowls and top with a sprinkling of the remaining parsley and some of the remaining bacon. Serve with the biscuits alongside.

TO GO: After adding the clam juice and fish stock, remove the soup from the heat. Add the warm milk and cream to the chowder off the heat. Pack the parsley and the bacon separately. At the party, gently reheat the chowder over low heat, being careful not to overcook the clams. Taste and adjust the seasoning, and sprinkle with remaining bacon and parsley before serving.

MAINE LOBSTER, LEEK, AND CORN CHOWDER

MAKES 12 TO 14 TASTING PORTIONS OR 8 TO 10 FULL SERVINGS

Many lobster chowders call for cooked lobster meat. But, I thought, why not cook the lobster in fish stock so you have an extra-flavorful lobster-infused stock to use for the chowder? After you cook the lobster in the stock, you cut it into generous bite-size pieces and then return it to the stock with sautéed leeks, potatoes, and chives. If you're making this soup in the summer, fresh corn on the cob is a wonderful addition. However, if fresh corn is not in season, you should skip it; the soup is completely satisfying and delicious without it. Serve with Buttery Biscuits (page 155) or Skillet Corn Bread with Chive and Brown Butter (page 154).

8 cups [7.5 L] Fish Stock (page 33)

3½ lb [1.6 kg] live Maine lobsters

2 medium leeks

2 Tbsp unsalted butter

2 large Yukon gold potatoes, peeled and cut into ½-in [12-mm] cubes

½ cup [20 g] minced fresh chives

½ to ¾ cup [120 to 180 ml] heavy cream

3 to 4 ears fresh corn or 2½ to 3⅓ cups [350 to 465 g] frozen corn kernels

Sea salt

Freshly ground black pepper

Sweet Hungarian paprika for garnish

1. In a large stockpot over medium-high heat, bring the fish stock to a vigorous simmer. Very carefully remove the rubber bands from the lobster claws (the lobsters can pinch you, so pay attention). Place the lobsters, shell-side up, in the pot, cover, and cook for 5 minutes. Remove the lid, flip the lobsters, and cook for another 5 minutes. Turn off the heat. Using tongs, remove the lobsters and let cool. Working over a flat, rimmed dish, such as a pie plate, to catch any released juice, remove the meat from the claws and the tail and cut into generous bite-size pieces; reserve the lobster meat and the juice. Remove the legs (not the claws but the thin spiny legs on the body), cut in half, and reserve.

2. Trim off the dark green sections from the leeks and save for making vegetable stock. Halve the pale green and white sections. Rinse under cold running water, pat dry, and cut crosswise into thin pieces.

3. In another large stockpot over low heat, melt the butter. Add the leeks and cook, stirring occasionally, for 5 minutes. Add the potatoes and half of the chives and cook, stirring, for 2 minutes. Turn the heat to high, add the stock and reserved lobster juice, and bring to a boil. Turn the heat to low, cover, and cook for 10 to 12 minutes, or until the potatoes are just tender.

4. In a small nonreactive saucepan over low heat, bring the cream to a gentle simmer. Remove from the heat, add the lobster pieces and the leg pieces, and let steep for 3 minutes. Then, add the cream and lobster to the stock.

continued

5. If using fresh corn, shuck the ears, remove the silks, and trim off the ends so that you can stand the cob flat. Using a sharp knife and standing each cob on its end inside a large bowl, remove the kernels from the cob by working the knife straight down against the cob. Using the blunt side of the knife, scrape down the cob after the kernels have been removed to release the corn "milk." Repeat with the remaining ears. Add the corn kernels, corn milk, and 2 Tbsp chives to the pot; season with salt and pepper; and cook for 5 minutes, or until the soup simmers. Taste and adjust the seasoning, adding more salt and pepper if needed.

6. Ladle the chowder into mugs or bowls and garnish with the remaining 2 Tbsp chives and the paprika before serving.

TO GO: Cook the chowder; add the lobster, cream, and corn; and immediately remove it from the heat. Pack the chives and paprika separately. At the party, carefully warm the chowder over low heat just until it simmers to prevent overcooking the lobster.

SCOTTISH-STYLE SMOKED HADDOCK AND LEEK CHOWDER

MAKES 8 TO 10 TASTING PORTIONS OR 6 TO 8 FULL SERVINGS

My friends Rebecca Mitchell and Ben Harris brought this chowder, known in Scotland as Cullen Skink, to one of our soup suppers and we went nuts for the smoky-sweet, delicate flavor. They found the original recipe in a British edition of *Country Living* magazine. My adaptation calls for smoked haddock, also called finnan haddie, which is widely available. This is a very rich chowder, so a little goes a long way. Serve with Buttery Biscuits (page 155).

2½ cups [600 ml] milk

1 lb [455 g] smoked haddock

1 bay leaf

3 or 4 sprigs fresh parsley

1 small onion, quartered

Freshly ground black pepper

2 medium leeks

1 Tbsp olive oil

1 Tbsp butter

Sea salt

2 Tbsp all-purpose flour

2 cups [480 ml] Fish Stock (page 33)

1 lb [455 g] potatoes, such as Yukon gold, peeled and diced

½ cup plus 2 Tbsp [150 ml] heavy cream, at room temperature

2 Tbsp minced fresh chives

1. In a medium stockpot over low heat, combine the milk, haddock, bay leaf, parsley, and onion; season with pepper; and bring to a simmer. Remove from the heat and let steep for 15 minutes to allow the smoked fish and the aromatics to flavor the milk. When cool enough to handle, remove the haddock from the milk and flake the meat, removing the skin and any bones, and set aside.

2. Trim off the dark green sections from the leeks and save for making vegetable stock. Halve the pale green and white sections lengthwise. Rinse under cold running water, pat dry, and cut crosswise into very thin pieces.

3. In a large stockpot over low heat, warm the olive oil and butter. Add the leeks, season with salt and pepper, and stir. Cover the pot and "sweat" the leeks, stirring once or twice, for 8 minutes. Stir in the flour and cook for 1 minute. Using a fine-mesh sieve, strain the milk over the pot and stir until well blended; discard the aromatics from the milk. Add the fish stock and bring to a gentle simmer; continue to simmer for 2 minutes. Add the potatoes, cover, and cook for 15 minutes, or until the potatoes are almost tender. Add the reserved haddock and the cream, turn the heat to very low, and simmer very gently for another 10 minutes, being careful not to let the soup boil. Taste and adjust the seasoning, adding more salt and pepper if needed.

4. Ladle the chowder into mugs or bowls, and sprinkle with the chives just before serving.

TO GO: Pack the chives separately.

SIDE DISHES

Soup can be filling, and sampling four, five, even six different types of soup at a soup-swap party can be even more so. Given this scenario, you want your side dishes to be light and fresh. You don't need to feel like you're being "lazy" by serving a simple bowl of mixed seasonal greens. After all, soup is the star at soup-swap suppers. But you can certainly get a bit more creative. Here are a few favorite salads and side dishes that have been big hits at our soup swaps. Almost all of them can be made ahead of time.

HERBED RICOTTA TOASTS
WITH SLOW-ROASTED CHERRY TOMATOES

MAKES 8 SERVINGS (2 TOASTS PER PERSON)

This is the most delicious open-faced grilled cheese and tomato sandwich imaginable. You slow-roast the tomatoes and mix the ricotta beforehand and then assemble the toasts just minutes before you're ready to serve. It makes a great first course or a side dish to any soup.

SLOW-ROASTED CHERRY TOMATOES

1½ lb [680 g] yellow, red, and orange cherry tomatoes or any mixture thereof

3 Tbsp olive oil

3 garlic cloves, chopped

1 Tbsp chopped fresh basil

1 Tbsp chopped fresh thyme

Sea salt

Freshly ground black pepper

HERBED RICOTTA

1¼ cups [300 g] whole-milk ricotta cheese

1 Tbsp olive oil

1 Tbsp chopped fresh thyme

1 Tbsp chopped fresh basil

1 Tbsp chopped fresh chives

Sea salt

Freshly ground black pepper

TOASTS

Sixteen ½-in- [12-mm-] thick slices crusty baguette

1½ Tbsp olive oil

1. **TO ROAST THE TOMATOES:** Position a rack in the middle of the oven and preheat to 225°F [110°C].

2. Place the tomatoes in an ovenproof skillet or shallow gratin dish. Add the olive oil, garlic, basil, and thyme; season with salt and pepper; and toss gently until the tomatoes are evenly coated. Roast for 1 to 1½ hours, or until the tomatoes begin to burst and are very soft, but not falling apart.

3. **TO PREPARE THE RICOTTA:** In a small bowl, combine the ricotta, olive oil, thyme, basil, and chives; season with salt and pepper; and mix gently. Cover and refrigerate until ready to use.

4. **TO MAKE THE TOASTS:** Preheat the broiler.

5. Arrange the baguette slices in a single layer on a large baking sheet. Using half of the olive oil, lightly brush one side of each slice and broil for 2 minutes, or until just golden brown and toasted. Remove from the oven. Flip the bread, brush with the remaining oil, and broil for 1 minute. Remove from the oven.

6. Spoon an equal amount of the ricotta mixture onto each toast, top with several roasted tomatoes, and drizzle with a bit of the juice from the dish. Broil for another 1 to 2 minutes, or until the cheese just begins to bubble. Serve hot or at room temperature with any remaining roasted tomatoes in a bowl on the side for guests to help themselves.

CROSTADA WITH BUTTERNUT, RED ONION, AND FETA

MAKES 8 SERVINGS

This savory crostada, which contains thin slices of orange butternut squash, red onion, and tangy feta cheese wrapped in a buttery thyme-flecked crust, is a great accompaniment to virtually any soup. It can be made several hours ahead and served at room temperature.

DOUGH

2 cups [280 g] unbleached all-purpose flour

Pinch of sea salt

1½ tsp chopped fresh thyme

1 cup [220 g] butter, well chilled and cut into ½-in- [12-mm-] thick pieces

⅓ cup [80 ml] ice water

1½ Tbsp olive oil

2 medium red onions, thinly sliced

1 small butternut squash, peeled, seeded, and cut into ½-in- [12-mm-] thick slices

2 Tbsp minced fresh chives

Sea salt

Freshly ground black pepper

½ cup [40 g] freshly grated Parmesan cheese

1 cup [80 g] feta cheese, crumbled

1. **TO MAKE THE DOUGH:** Using a food processor fitted with the metal blade, mix together the flour, salt, and thyme. Add the butter and pulse about fifteen times, or until the mixture is the consistency of coarse cornmeal. With the motor running, slowly add just enough of the ice water to hold the dough together, stopping when the dough begins to pull away from the sides of the bowl.

2. Form the dough into a ball and place in plastic wrap. Refrigerate for at least 2 hours, or up to overnight.

3. In a large skillet over low heat, warm the olive oil. Add the onions and cook, stirring, for 8 minutes. Add the squash and the chives, season with salt and pepper, and cook, stirring, for 12 to 14 minutes, or until the squash is just tender when tested with a small, sharp knife. Taste and adjust the seasoning, adding more salt and pepper as needed. Remove from the heat and let cool.

4. Working on a well-floured surface, roll out the dough to form a 14-in [35.5-cm] circle and place on a baking sheet. Sprinkle the dough with ¼ cup [20 g] of the Parmesan, ½ cup [40 g] of the feta, and a generous grinding of pepper. Arrange the squash and onions in a circle, leaving a 2-in [5-cm] border around the circumference of the dough. Sprinkle the remaining ¼ cup [20 g] Parmesan and ½ cup [40 g] feta on top. Drape the bare edge of the dough up around the filling, creating "pleats" and pressing them into place, leaving about 6 in [15 cm] of the filling in the center uncovered by the dough. Chill the crostada in the refrigerator for 30 minutes.

5. Position a rack in the middle of the oven and preheat to 425°F [220°C].

6. Bake the crostada for 30 to 45 minutes, or until the pastry is a rich golden brown and the cheese is bubbling. Remove from the oven and let cool for just a few minutes. Serve hot or at room temperature.

SKILLET CORN BREAD
WITH CHIVE AND BROWN BUTTER

MAKES 8 SERVINGS

This is an old favorite—corn bread baked directly in a cast-iron or heavy ovenproof skillet with brown butter, chives, and creamy buttermilk. After baking the bread for 15 minutes, you pour additional milk on top to create a custardy layer. Although this is essentially a savory corn bread, you can control how much sugar you add; ¼ cup [50 g] gives you just a hint of sweetness.

2½ Tbsp lightly salted butter

3 Tbsp minced fresh chives

1½ cups [175 g] cornmeal

¼ to ½ cup [50 to 100 g] sugar

½ cup [60 g] all-purpose flour

1 tsp sea salt

½ tsp baking soda

1 cup [240 ml] buttermilk

2 eggs, lightly beaten

2 cups [480 ml] whole milk

Sweet butter and honey for serving
    (optional)

1. Position a rack in the middle of the oven and preheat to 350°F [165°C].

2. In a 10-in [25-cm] ovenproof skillet (preferably cast iron) over medium-high heat, melt the butter. As soon as the butter just begins to brown, remove the skillet from the heat and add the chives.

3. In a large bowl, whisk the cornmeal, sugar, flour, salt, and baking soda until well blended. Add the buttermilk and eggs and whisk to combine. Whisk in 1 cup [240 ml] of the whole milk. Add 2 Tbsp of the chive-brown butter, leaving the remainder in the skillet, and whisk until combined. Pour the batter into the skillet and bake for 15 minutes.

4. Pour the remaining 1 cup [240 ml] milk on top of the bread and bake for another 25 to 35 minutes, or until the corn bread is golden brown and firm. When you gently shake the skillet, the corn bread shouldn't wobble but it doesn't need to be bone dry when tested with a toothpick in the center. Remove and let cool slightly. Serve warm, with butter and honey if desired.

BUTTERY BISCUITS

MAKES 10 BISCUITS

A fresh-from-the-oven biscuit is a good companion for any soup or chowder. You can turn these into herb biscuits by working a handful of chopped fresh chives, basil, thyme, and/or rosemary into the dough.

1½ cups plus 3 Tbsp [210 g]
    all-purpose flour
1 Tbsp baking powder
1 Tbsp sugar
½ tsp sea salt
½ cup [110 g] butter, chilled and cut
    into small pieces
½ cup [120 ml] whole milk

1. Position a rack in the middle of the oven and preheat to 375°F [190°C].

2. In a large bowl, sift together the flour, baking powder, sugar, and salt. Add the butter and, using your hands or a pastry blender, gently work the butter into the mixture until it resembles coarse cornmeal. Add the milk and mix until the dough just comes together, being careful not to over-mix.

3. Place the dough on a clean, well-floured surface and knead it gently for a few minutes. Roll out the dough to a thickness of ½ in [12 mm]. This is important; if you roll it out too thin your biscuits will be flat and dry, and if you roll it out too thick they won't bake properly. Using a biscuit cutter or a small water glass that is 2 in [5 cm] in diameter, cut out ten biscuits and place them on an ungreased baking sheet. To get all ten biscuits, you may need to cut out eight or nine and then reroll the scraps.

4. Bake for 16 to 18 minutes, or until the biscuits are golden brown and slightly risen. Serve hot.

MIXED GREENS SALAD
WITH MINT-TANGERINE VINAIGRETTE

MAKES 8 SERVINGS

Fresh mint leaves are scattered throughout the salad and then chopped into the vinaigrette, giving the salad a bright, fresh, almost summery flavor. Full of great textures, flavors, and color, this salad is ideal for any season. It adds a refreshing counterpoint to virtually any soup in this book.

MINT-TANGERINE VINAIGRETTE

2 tsp Dijon mustard

¼ cup [15 g] packed stemmed and coarsely chopped mint

Sea salt

Freshly ground black pepper

2 scallions, finely chopped

½ cup [120 ml] fresh tangerine, orange, or blood orange juice

2 Tbsp white wine vinegar

⅔ cup [160 ml] olive oil

SALAD

8 oz [230 g] mixed greens (I use a mix of baby greens, arugula, and chopped romaine)

1 large fennel bulb, fronds removed and bulb very thinly sliced

2 cups [110 g] fresh mint leaves, stemmed and roughly torn into large pieces

4 scallions, finely chopped

12 radishes, very thinly sliced

2 tangerines, peeled, halved lengthwise (unless they are very small, in which case you can leave them whole), seeds removed, and cut into ½-in [12-mm] pieces

16 pitted dried dates, cut into slivers

1 cup [110 g] pecan halves, toasted (see page 60)

1. **TO MAKE THE VINAIGRETTE:** In a small bowl, combine the mustard and mint and season with salt and pepper. Add the scallions, tangerine juice, and vinegar. Add the olive oil in a slow, steady stream, whisking until blended. Taste and adjust the seasoning, adding more salt and pepper if needed. (Store, covered, in the refrigerator for up to 5 days.)

2. **TO MAKE THE SALAD:** Place the greens in a large salad bowl or on a platter. Randomly scatter the fennel, mint, scallions, radishes, tangerine pieces, dates, and toasted pecans over the greens or add them one by one in layers.

3. Just before serving, toss the salad with a little more than half the vinaigrette; serve the remaining vinaigrette on the side.

BURNT RADICCHIO SALAD
WITH HERBED RICOTTA AND NUTS

MAKES 6 TO 8 SERVINGS

El Rey Luncheonette is a tiny café on the Lower East Side of Manhattan that is filled with hipsters in flannel shirts and long, exotic beards. This is my take on their exceptional Burnt Radicchio Salad. Radicchio, a type of Italian chicory with a pleasing sharp bite, is roasted until crisp and then served with whipped herbed ricotta, honey, grated lemon zest, and nuts. The radicchio can be roasted a day ahead, and the recipe can easily be doubled. Toast the nuts (see page 60) if you have time. To make honey pourable, heat it in a microwave for about 20 seconds or heat the glass jar in a small pot of simmering water. The bitter radicchio is a great complement to many rich soups.

2 small heads radicchio, each cored and cut into 6 wedges

2½ Tbsp olive oil

Sea salt

Freshly ground black pepper

1 cup [240 g] fresh whole-milk ricotta cheese

1½ tsp freshly grated lemon zest, plus more for garnish

2 Tbsp minced fresh chives

½ cup [60 g] chopped hazelnuts, cashews, or almonds

¼ cup [85 g] honey

1. Position a rack in the middle of the oven and preheat to 475°F [245°C].

2. Place the radicchio in a medium roasting pan or 8-in [20-cm] ovenproof skillet, drizzle with the olive oil, and season with salt and pepper. Roast for 15 to 20 minutes, or until the edges are just beginning to crisp up (just short of burning) and the color is deepened. Remove from the oven and let cool.

3. Meanwhile, in a small bowl, combine the ricotta, lemon zest, and chives and season with salt and pepper.

4. Smear the ricotta mixture on a serving plate (you can use an offset spatula for this), top with the radicchio, and sprinkle with the nuts. Drizzle the honey over the radicchio and top with just a pinch of grated lemon zest and pepper. Serve immediately.

RED CABBAGE SALAD
WITH BLUE CHEESE AND MAPLE-GLAZED WALNUTS

MAKES 8 SERVINGS

Red cabbage is thinly sliced and tossed with tangy blue cheese and sweet maple-glazed walnuts. To slice the cabbage quickly, core it first, cut it into wedges, and then slice in a food processor or by hand. You can also use a mandolin if you have one.

VINAIGRETTE
2 Tbsp crumbled blue cheese
1 scallion, very thinly sliced
½ cup [120 ml] olive oil
¼ cup [60 ml] red or white wine vinegar
1 Tbsp Dijon mustard
Sea salt
Freshly ground black pepper

WALNUTS
1½ tsp butter
1 Tbsp olive oil
1 cup [110 g] walnuts
Sea salt
Freshly ground black pepper
3 Tbsp pure maple syrup

8 cups [500 g] very thinly sliced red cabbage, or a mixture of red and white cabbage
2 scallions, very thinly sliced
⅓ cup [30 g] crumbled blue cheese

1. **TO MAKE THE VINAIGRETTE:** In a small bowl, use the back of a kitchen spoon to mash 1 Tbsp of the blue cheese into a paste. Stir in the remaining 1 Tbsp blue cheese, the scallion, olive oil, vinegar, and mustard. Season with salt and pepper and stir until well blended. Set aside.

2. **TO MAKE THE WALNUTS:** Place a piece of parchment or wax paper next to the stove. In a medium skillet over medium heat, melt the butter with the olive oil. Add the walnuts and cook, stirring, for 2 minutes. Season with salt and pepper, drizzle with the maple syrup, and cook, stirring, for 4 to 5 minutes, until the nuts are evenly coated and have begun to caramelize. Transfer the nuts to the parchment, spooning any excess syrup from the skillet over them, and let cool. Be sure to separate the nuts while they're still warm.

3. On a large platter or in a salad bowl, toss the cabbage and scallions. Spoon half of the vinaigrette over the salad and toss well. Top with the blue cheese and walnuts. Serve immediately, with the remaining vinaigrette on the side.

CITRUS SALAD
WITH CRÈME FRAÎCHE AND TARRAGON

MAKES 6 TO 8 SERVINGS

The variety of fresh citrus found during the winter months—blood oranges, oranges, tangerines, grapefruit—is such a treat. This sweet, citrus-based salad goes well with any soup, particularly a hearty soup that needs a little something light to brighten up a meal. You can use any variety of citrus you can find, but the more the merrier. Some people think this salad can also serve as dessert, since it's so naturally sweet and refreshing.

2 blood oranges

2 tangerines or satsuma (mandarin) oranges

1 cup [30 g] arugula

⅓ to ½ cup [80 to 120 ml] crème fraîche or plain Greek yogurt

1½ Tbsp chopped fresh tarragon

CITRUS-TARRAGON VINAIGRETTE

1 Tbsp chopped fresh tarragon

¼ cup [60 ml] white wine vinegar

Reserved citrus juice

Sea salt

Freshly ground black pepper

½ cup [120 ml] olive oil

1. Working over a bowl to catch any released citrus juice, remove the rind from the oranges and tangerines. Without separating them into sections, cut the citrus crosswise into ½-in- [12-mm-] thick "wheels." Remove the seeds and reserve the juice.

2. On a serving platter, spread out the arugula. Top with the citrus slices, alternating colors and variety. Then top with small dollops of the crème fraîche and sprinkle with the tarragon.

3. **TO MAKE THE VINAIGRETTE:** Add the tarragon and vinegar to the reserved citrus juice and season with salt and pepper. Add the olive oil in a slow, steady stream, whisking until well blended.

4. Drizzle the salad with the vinaigrette before serving, or pass both separately.

GARNISHES & TOPPINGS

Sometimes the simplest ingredient can bring out big flavors in a soup. This chapter offers quick, easy ideas for garnishes (in addition to the garnish ideas listed in the individual recipes) as well as a variety of toppings that work well in all kinds of soups.

Toppings add flavor dimension, texture, and color to soup. I'm not talking about a slice of bread floating like a soggy sponge that's about to sink into your soup. No. Consider instead a drizzle of bright green herb-flavored oil or a crunchy bread-crumb-and-herb topping. What about a few crunchy slices of Quick Pickled Radishes, a dollop of Avocado Crema, a splash of extra-virgin olive oil, or a sprinkle of fried whole herb leaves? Try swirling a teaspoon of Miso Butter or Parsley Pesto into your hot soup and watch what happens. Crispy Croutes, Double-Cheese Croutes, and Polenta Croutons are a few other possibilities. Almost all of these toppings can be made ahead and are quick and simple to prepare. And they can take a simple bowl of soup to a whole new level. What are you waiting for?

Garnishes: Ideas for Toppings, Crunch, Color, Flavor, Pow!

- **A few drops of lemon oil, orange oil, or any herb-infused oil** will bring out new flavors in your soup. Citrus oils can be found in specialty food shops or you can make your own by combining olive oil with grated zest and gently warming over low heat for 10 minutes. Then remove from the heat and let steep for several hours. Use a clean, sterilized eyedropper to add just a few drops to finished soups as a garnish. Even a tiny drizzle of very fruity extra-virgin olive oil will add a delicious finish to soups. Think about adding citrus oil to Greek-Style Turkey and Rice Soup with Meyer Lemon and Dill, Sicilian Black Lentil Soup with Guanciale and Grated Orange, or Pork and White Bean Chili.

- **Grated citrus zest**—think lemon and Meyer lemon but also tangerine, grapefruit, lime, or orange—can really wake up the flavor of vegetable-, seafood-, or meat-based soups such as Lamb and Lentil Soup with Lamb Meatballs, Corn and Sweet-Potato Chowder with Saffron Cream, or Chorizo and Clam Stew with Tomatoes and Arugula.

- **Candied ginger** cut into very thin strips adds the bracing bite of ginger and a touch of sweetness. Try a few thin slices on Roasted Carrot and Ginger Soup or Thai Red Curry–Chicken Noodle Soup.

- **Toasted coarsely chopped nuts**—from walnuts, almonds, and hazelnuts to pistachios and pine nuts—add wonderful flavor as well as texture. (See page 60 for tips on toasting nuts.) Toasted chopped nuts would serve as a delicious counterpoint to the creamy texture and earthy flavor of Chestnut Soup with Mushroom-Thyme Sauté or California Cream of Artichoke Soup.

- **Cooked and crumbled pancetta or bacon** adds a meaty dimension to vegetable-based soups. Try it on top of Asparagus and Leek Soup with Poached Egg, "No-Cream" Cream of Celery Root Soup with Fried Capers, or Minestrone Soup.

- **Grated or thinly sliced cheese**—hard cheeses like Parmesan and Gruyère as well as crumbled soft goat cheese, ricotta, and feta—add richness and smoothness. Grate some cheese on Sausage, Cabbage, and Root Vegetable Soup; Hope's Italian Sausage–Zucchini Soup; or Italian Wedding Soup.

- **Hard-boiled eggs** make a great garnish and add richness and color to vegetable soups, bean soups, or tomato soup. Cut the cooked egg in half and force it through a fine-mesh sieve to create small bits of white and yolk to sprinkle on each bowl of soup. Sprinkle it on Late-Spring Pea and Lettuce Soup or Black

Bean and Chorizo Soup with Avocado Crema for a creative touch.

- Float **a spoonful of fresh crabmeat** (or cooked lobster cut into small chunks) in the center of vegetable soups for an unexpected visual as well as flavor accent. California Cream of Artichoke Soup and Late-Spring Pea and Lettuce Soup are good candidates.

- Get creative and whip up some **Parmesan Cheese Crisps** (page 168), a simple and fast topping that adds drama to Minestrone; Roasted Fall-Vegetable Soup; or Portuguese-Style Kale, White Bean, and Chorizo Soup.

- Add a cooling flavor and extra richness—not to mention color in the case of some soups—with **a dollop of crème fraîche or plain Greek yogurt**. Drop 1 tsp on Potato-Leek Soup with Chive Oil, Roasted Carrot and Ginger Soup, or Beef-Barley Mushroom Soup.

- Sprinkle each serving with the **chopped fresh herbs** that were used to flavor the soup—minced fresh chives or chopped fresh basil, rosemary, thyme, lemon verbena, etc. Don't use dried herbs unless called for; they won't add much oomph!

- **Microgreens** add color and texture and freshen the flavor of soups, particularly rich, puréed ones. Microgreens are found in specialty food shops or some well-stocked grocery stores. They are the shoots of greens and vegetables such as Swiss chard, beets, mustard greens, and arugula that are picked when they are tiny and young and very tender. Sprinkle microgreens on Potato-Leek Soup with Chive Oil or California Cream of Artichoke Soup.

- **Roasted Chickpeas** (page 170) add crunch and flavor. And they make a great snack for later too.

- **A dab of harissa** (Tunisian hot chili paste) adds a kick to any soup that begs for a spicy, smoky flavor.

- **A spoonful of salsa or hot-pepper sauce** will liven up any soup, particularly bean-based soups and chilis.

- **Pomegranate seeds** add color, crunch, and fruity flavor to puréed soups and vegetable soups. Their gorgeous maroon/red color will leach into the soup, so make sure you're prepared for that.

- For a Provençal accent, add **a dab of tapenade or pitted finely chopped green and/or black olives**. Try this with Tomato Soup with Grilled-Cheese Croutons, Roasted Fall-Vegetable Soup, or Minestrone Soup.

- For wonderful color and a hint of sweetness, you can't beat **finely chopped or thinly sliced roasted red, yellow, or green bell peppers**. Try adding some to Roasted Pumpkin Soup with Fried Sage Leaves or Escarole and White Bean Soup with Parmesan Cheese.

- **Chopped or slivered sun-dried tomatoes** add color and a bit of acidity to any soup that already has tomato as an ingredient.

AVOCADO CREMA

MAKES ABOUT 1 CUP [240 ML]

This delicious, creamy puree of avocados, spices, lime juice, and sour cream tastes so sophisticated you won't believe how quick it is to put together. Use it top bean soups, chilis, or soups with a Latin flavor.

1 large, ripe but not mushy avocado, peeled, pitted, and cut into large chunks
¾ tsp ground cumin
2½ tsp fresh lime juice
2 tsp sour cream
1 tsp finely chopped cilantro
Sea salt
Freshly ground black pepper

In a small bowl, finely mash the avocado with a fork. Add the cumin, lime juice, sour cream, and cilantro; season with salt and pepper; and stir, making sure that all the ingredients are evenly incorporated. The crema will be thick and chunky. Serve immediately or place a piece of plastic wrap or wax paper directly on the surface of the crema to prevent discoloration and refrigerate for up to 4 hours.

MISO BUTTER

MAKES ABOUT 3 TBSP

A simple miso-flavored butter adds a meaty, full umami flavor to soups, particularly vegetable-based ones like Baby Turnip Soup (see page 61), Asparagus and Leek Soup (see page 44), Late-Fall Vegetable Ramen (see page 40), or Miso Soup (see page 49).

2½ Tbsp unsalted butter
1 Tbsp white miso or your favorite miso paste

In a small saucepan over low heat, melt the butter. Stir in the miso and heat until the mixture is well blended and forms a smooth paste. You can use the butter when it is hot or at room temperature. Cover and refrigerate for up to 1 week.

CHIVE OIL

MAKES ABOUT ¾ CUP [180 ML]

This emerald-green oil adds a subtle onion flavor and gorgeous color to vegetable and seafood soups. I like keeping it in one of those squeeze bottles that diners use to serve mustard and ketchup, so that I can drizzle it on top of hot or cold soups. (You may need to enlarge the opening, as bits of chives can get stuck.)

The oil adds great depth of flavor and color to Potato-Leek Soup (see page 43), "No Cream" Cream of Celery Root Soup (see page 55), and Parsnip and Cauliflower "Vichyssoise" (see page 42). You can make this oil using basil, thyme, lemon verbena, parsley, or your favorite fresh herb.

¾ cup [45 g] packed chopped fresh chives
¾ cup [180 ml] olive oil
Sea salt
Freshly ground black pepper

Using a food processor or blender, purée the chives and olive oil; season with salt and pepper. Store in a covered container in the refrigerator for up to 1 week. Bring to room temperature before serving.

GREMOLATA

MAKES ½ CUP [40 G]

Why would anyone want to put bread crumbs on top of soup? Just think about it. Croutons are essentially just big bread crumbs. This mixture of crunchy panko bread crumbs, lemon zest, chives, and parsley, however, adds surprisingly rich flavor as well as texture to many soups. This mixture is especially good on puréed soups like Parsnip and Cauliflower "Vichyssoise" (see page 42), "No-Cream" Cream of Celery Root Soup (see page 55), and other puréed soups.

1 Tbsp butter
1 Tbsp olive oil
½ cup [40 g] panko (Japanese bread crumbs)
Sea salt
Freshly ground black pepper
1 tsp finely fresh lemon zest
1 Tbsp finely chopped fresh parsley
1 Tbsp minced fresh chives

1. In a small saucepan over low heat, melt the butter. Add the olive oil and stir to combine. Add the panko and toss until the crumbs are completely coated. Toast the crumbs, stirring constantly, for 3 to 5 minutes, until they are golden brown. Season with salt and pepper and toss to combine. Remove from the heat and let cool for about 10 minutes.

2. Add the lemon zest, parsley, and chives to the crumb mixture and toss to combine. Store in an airtight container in the refrigerator for up to 2 days.

PARSLEY PESTO

MAKES ABOUT ¾ CUP [180 G]

Parsley can be much more than a garnish, as this vibrant green pesto demonstrates. Made with parsley instead of traditional basil, this pesto is ideal for winter, when fresh herbs are scarce. Serve it with any puréed or chunky vegetable soup for a fresh, rich herb flavor. Use freshly grated Parmesan, Romano, manchego, or your favorite hard cheese.

1 cup [60 g] packed chopped fresh parsley leaves
½ cup [65 g] walnuts, almonds, pistachios, or pine nuts, toasted (see page 60; optional)
1 garlic clove, peeled
Sea salt
Freshly ground black pepper
½ cup [120 ml] olive oil
¼ cup [15 g] packed freshly grated hard cheese (see headnote)

Using a food processor or blender, process the parsley, nuts (if using), and garlic until finely chopped and season with salt

continued

and pepper. With the motor running, add the olive oil in a slow, steady stream, being careful not to overprocess the pesto; it should still be a little chunky. Transfer to a bowl and stir in the cheese. Taste and adjust the seasoning, adding more salt and pepper if needed. Store in an airtight container in the refrigerator for up to 3 days or in the freezer for up to 4 months. Bring to room temperature before serving.

FRIED SAGE OR PARSLEY

MAKES ENOUGH TO
GARNISH 8 SERVINGS

You can use this technique—frying whole leaves in hot oil—with any type of fresh herb, but sage and parsley work particularly well. The herbs must be free of any grit and thoroughly dry before frying. Sage leaves make a particularly good topping for pumpkin or squash soups, and fried parsley goes with just about anything but is especially delicious with Spring Parsley-Watercress Soup (page 54), Minestrone Soup (page 74), or Hope's Italian Sausage-Zucchini Soup (page 110).

The best way to make these fried sage leaves is on the spot, but unless the party is at your house, it's difficult to do so; you don't want to be taking up precious space on the stove when there are all those soups to be heated.

1 oz [30 g] fresh sage or parsley leaves
**2 to 3 cups [480 to 720 ml] olive or safflower oil (or a
    combination of both)**
Sea salt

1. Carefully snip off the short, thin stems from the main stems of the sage, leaving the leaves attached, and set aside. For parsley you can trim the stem a bit but keep most of it attached to the leaves.

2. In a heavy medium skillet over medium-high heat, warm the olive oil until it just begins to smoke. Using tongs, very carefully lower the herbs into the hot oil, adding only a few at a time to avoid crowding the skillet and thereby lowering the temperature of the oil. (The oil is hot enough when the leaves immediately begin to sizzle.) Fry the leaves for about 15 seconds, then carefully flip them and fry for another 15 seconds, or until they are beginning to turn golden brown. Using a slotted spoon, transfer the leaves as they finish frying and drain on paper towels or on a clean brown grocery bag. Season with salt. Don't fry more than 15 minutes ahead of serving them, or the leaves will wilt.

FRIED CAPERS

MAKES ½ CUP [120 G]

I love using these piquant, salty, crunchy buds as a topping for puréed soups, particularly "No-Cream" Cream of Celery Root Soup (see page 55). They are also delicious on salads, and they are great accompaniments for cheese plates.

If using salt-packed capers, you must rinse them thoroughly under cold running water to remove the salt and thoroughly dry them.

1½ Tbsp olive oil
½ cup [120 g] nonpareil capers, drained and dried

In a medium skillet over medium heat, warm the olive oil until hot but not smoking. (A caper or a speck of bread crumb should sizzle when the oil is hot enough.) Using a slotted spoon, carefully add the capers a few at a time to avoid crowding the skillet, and cook, stirring, for 3 to 4 minutes, until they are evenly browned. They should be crisp and hot. Using the spoon, transfer them to paper towels to drain. Serve hot.

TO GO: You can fry the capers about 1 hour ahead and wrap them in paper towels for transport, but they don't keep their crunch after 10 minutes or so.

ROUILLE

MAKES ABOUT 1 CUP [240 G]

Rouille is a thick Provençal sauce that is made from bread, saffron, chili powder, and lots of garlic. It is traditionally served as a condiment with bouillabaisse and other fish soups. I like to make it without chili powder because I don't want it to overwhelm the soup. But if you want some heat, add a pinch.

1 large red bell pepper
2 cups [70 g] chopped crusty day-old bread
2 garlic cloves, chopped
½ cup [120 ml] olive oil
Pinch of saffron
Pinch of chili powder or cayenne pepper (optional)
Sea salt
Freshly ground black pepper

1. If you have a gas stove, turn one of the burners to high. Place the bell pepper directly on top of the flame and char the skin, flipping it from side to side, for about 8 minutes, or until evenly blackened. Alternatively, preheat the broiler. Place the bell pepper on a piece of aluminum foil or a baking sheet and broil, turning it a few times, for about 8 minutes, or until evenly blackened. Using tongs, immediately place the blackened pepper in a paper bag, fold over the top a few times, and let steam for about 2 minutes. Remove the pepper from the bag and peel off the blackened skin. Discard the core and seeds and chop the flesh.

2. Using a food processor fitted with the steel blade, chop the bread finely until it looks like coarse bread crumbs. Add the garlic and roasted pepper and chop until blended. Add the olive oil, saffron, and chili powder (if using); season with salt and pepper; and process until the sauce is thick and chunky. Taste and adjust the seasoning, adding more salt and pepper if needed. Store in an airtight container in the refrigerator for up to 2 days. Bring to room temperature before serving.

CROUTES

MAKES 8 CROUTES

The term *croute* refers to toasted slices of crusty bread that have been cut into oversize croutons. They add a pleasant crunch and make a great topping for virtually any soup in this book.

Eight ¼- to ½-in- [6- to 12-mm-] thick slices of baguette, *ciabatta*, or any other crusty bread
2 Tbsp olive oil

continued

1. Preheat the broiler.

2. Arrange the bread slices in a single layer on a baking sheet. Using half of the olive oil, lightly brush one side of each slice and broil for about 1 minute, or until golden brown. Remove from the broiler and flip the bread. Brush with the remaining oil and broil for another minute or so, until the second side is golden brown. Let cool and store in an airtight container at room temperature for up to 4 hours.

TO GO: Pack the croutes in a metal cookie tin or tightly sealed plastic container, placing a piece of paper towel between layers so that the croutes don't sit on top of one another and get soggy.

|||||||||||||||||||||||||||||||||||||||||||||||||||||||||||||

DOUBLE-CHEESE CROUTES

MAKES 12 CROUTES

These crisp, cheesy croutes are the perfect topping for **Roasted Fall-Vegetable Soup (page 63), French Onion Soup (see page 71), or any soup where the flavor of cheese and the crunch of toast will work.**

Twelve ¼- to ½-in- [6- to 12-mm-] thick slices of baguette, or any other crusty bread
4 Tbsp [60 ml] olive oil
1 cup [80 g] freshly grated Parmesan, Gruyère, Swiss, cheddar, manchego, soft goat, blue, or any cheese you prefer

1. Position an oven rack as close to the heating element in the broiler as you can and preheat.

2. Arrange the bread slices in a single layer on a baking sheet. Using half of the olive oil, lightly brush one side of each slice and broil for 1 to 2 minutes, or until just beginning to turn golden brown. Remove from the broiler, sprinkle with ½ cup [40 g] of the cheese, and broil for another 1 to 2 minutes, or until the cheese is melted. Remove from the broiler, and let cool.

3. Using tongs, gently flip the bread. Brush with the remaining oil and broil for 1 to 2 minutes, until golden brown. Remove from the broiler, sprinkle with the remaining ½ cup [40 g] cheese, and broil for another minute, or until the cheese is melted. Let cool. Store in an airtight container at room temperature for up to 1 day.

TO GO: Pack the croutes in a metal cookie tin or tightly sealed plastic container, placing a piece of paper towel between layers so that the croutes don't sit on top of one another and get soggy.

|||||||||||||||||||||||||||||||||||||||||||||||||||||||||||||

PARMESAN CHEESE CRISPS

MAKES ABOUT 12 CRISPS

Recipes don't get much simpler than this—one ingredient and about 10 minutes in the oven and they are ready to top a bowl of **Minestrone Soup (page 74) or Roasted Fall-Vegetable Soup (page 63).** These are thin, delicate cheese crisps.

1 cup [80 g] freshly grated Parmesan cheese

1. Preheat the oven to 350°F [180°C].

2. Drop heaping tablespoons of the grated cheese about 2 in [5 cm] apart on a Silpat- or parchment paper–lined baking sheet and bake for about 10 minutes; the cheese will not look melted and bubbling but the crisp should hold together. Remove from the oven and set aside to cool. Use a flat spatula to remove the disks from the sheet. Slip one or two on top of each bowl of soup.

TO GO: Pack the crisps in a tightly sealed plastic container, placing a piece of paper towel or parchment paper between layers to keep them safe while you travel. These are tough to keep crisp when there is humidity in the air. You may want to refrigerate or keep in a cool spot.

||||||||||||||||||||||||||||||||||||||||||||||||||||||||||||||||||||||||||||||

POLENTA CROUTONS

MAKES ABOUT 100 SMALL OR
72 MEDIUM CROUTONS

Where is it written that all croutons must be made from leftover bread? Why not experiment with squares of polenta to make cornmeal croutons? To save lots of time, you can buy precooked polenta logs (which are available in many supermarkets). Just cut them into tiny cubes, brush with olive oil, and broil on both sides as instructed in the recipe. These gluten-free croutons are great in chowders, vegetable soups, or any type of Italian or bean-based soup. You can also add freshly grated Parmesan cheese to the polenta just before you pour it onto the baking pan if you want a cheesy crouton.

5½ cups [1.3 L] water
Sea salt
4 Tbsp [60 ml] olive oil

1½ cups [210 g] instant polenta
Freshly ground black pepper
½ cup [40 g] freshly grated Parmesan or favorite hard cheese (optional)

1. In a large saucepan over high heat, bring the water to a boil. Add a pinch of salt and 1 Tbsp of the olive oil. In a slow, steady stream, pour the polenta into the boiling water, whisking as you add it. Turn the heat to low, season with salt and pepper, and cook, whisking, for 3 minutes. Remove from the heat, cover, and let sit for 5 minutes. Stir in the cheese (if using).

2. Grease a 16-by-12-in [40-by-30-cm] rimmed baking sheet or a 13-by-9-in [33-by-23-cm] baking pan with 1 Tbsp olive oil. Transfer the polenta to the pan. Using a large, flat spatula, spread out the polenta in an even layer and let cool to room temperature. Cover loosely with plastic wrap and refrigerate for about 1 hour, until chilled.

3. Preheat the broiler.

4. Cut the polenta into ½-in [12-mm] or 1-in [2.5-cm] cubes and place on a second rimmed baking sheet. Using a pastry brush or the back of a kitchen spoon, brush the polenta cubes with 1 Tbsp olive oil, and season with salt and pepper. Broil for 4 to 6 minutes, or until light golden brown and crisp. Remove the cubes from the oven, gently flip them, and brush with the remaining 1 Tbsp olive oil. Broil for another 3 minutes, or until golden and hot. Store in an airtight container in the refrigerator for up to 3 days. Reheat in a 400°F [200°C] oven for 5 minutes before serving.

TO GO: Pack the thoroughly cooled croutons in a tightly sealed plastic container, placing a piece of paper towel between layers so that the croutons don't sit on top of one another and get soggy.

GRILLED-CHEESE CROUTONS

MAKES 24 TO 32 CROUTONS

This new twist on the classic accompaniment to tomato soup will go well with almost any vegetable-based soup. You can use your favorite type of freshly grated hard cheese and any fresh herb you like to complement the soup you're serving.

8 bread slices of any variety you like
2½ Tbsp olive oil
8 fresh basil leaves
1 cup [80 g] freshly grated sharp cheddar, Parmesan, or other hard cheese

1. Preheat the broiler.

2. Arrange the bread slices in a single layer on a baking sheet. Using half of the olive oil, lightly brush one side of each slice and broil for 2 to 3 minutes, or until golden brown. Remove from the oven, flip the bread, and brush with the remaining oil. Top each slice with a basil leaf and sprinkle with an equal amount of cheese. Broil until the cheese is melted and bubbling.

3. When ready to serve, cut the bread in half and serve the crouton open-faced, or sandwich two pieces of bread together and cut each sandwich into six large or eight small croutons.

TO GO: The croutons can be made about 1 hour ahead, but they are best when made at the last minute. Be sure to cool them before packing them in a tightly sealed container for transport.

ROASTED CHICKPEAS

MAKES ABOUT 1 CUP [220 G]

Crunchy, chewy, and delicious on top of virtually any soup or salad.

1 cup cooked chickpeas or canned chickpeas (drained, rinsed, and re-drained)
1½ Tbsp olive oil
Sea salt
Freshly ground black pepper

1. Preheat the oven to 350°F [180°C]. Line a baking sheet with parchment paper.

2. Toss the chickpeas with the olive oil and season with salt and pepper. Spread the mixture onto the prepared baking sheet in a single layer and bake for 10 to 15 minutes, or until they crisp up, begin to pop, and turn golden brown. Let cool. Store in an airtight container at room temperature for up to 1 day.

MUSHROOM-THYME SAUTÉ

MAKES ABOUT 1 CUP [240 G]

Chose any type of mushroom you like—regular button, shiitake, cremini, portobello, porcini—or, better yet, a combination of several types of mushrooms. This garnish works well with Five-Mushroom Soup (see page 68), Roasted Pumpkin Soup (see page 66), Roasted Fall-Vegetable Soup (page 63), or any soup that would benefit from the meaty flavor of mushrooms.

1½ Tbsp olive oil
1 lb [455 g] coarsely chopped mushrooms (see headnote)
2 Tbsp chopped fresh thyme
Sea salt
Freshly ground black pepper
3½ Tbsp [55 ml] dry sherry

In a small skillet over low heat, warm the olive oil. Add the mushrooms and thyme, season with salt and pepper, and sauté, stirring, for about 3 minutes. Turn the heat to high, add the sherry, and cook for 2 minutes, or until the sherry has been absorbed by the mushrooms. Taste and adjust the seasoning, adding more salt and pepper if needed. Let cool. Store in an airtight container in the refrigerator for up to 4 hours. Bring to room temperature before serving.

TO GO: Bring a small ovenproof skillet or shallow-sided baking dish to reheat the mixture at the party in a 300°F [150°C] oven until hot.

QUICK PICKLED RADISHES

MAKES ABOUT ½ CUP [120 ML]

These pickles take about 15 minutes from start to finish. They are delicious in Black Bean and Chorizo Soup (see page 113) and Pork and White Bean Chili (page 132). You can also use them to perk up tacos or salads. The recipe can easily be doubled or tripled.

2 to 3 large radishes, sliced paper-thin
¼ cup [60 ml] apple cider vinegar
¼ cup [60 ml] water
Sea salt
Freshly ground black pepper

Place the radishes in a nonreactive bowl or glass jar, add the vinegar and water, and season with salt and pepper. Make sure the radishes are totally submerged in the liquid and set aside for 10 minutes. Drain and serve or store in an airtight container in the refrigerator for up to 1 week.

INDEX

ACKNOWLEDGMENTS

I am grateful to many people for the making of this book. Oddly, I would also like to thank winter. As much as I resist you year after year, you are the true inspiration for making warm, comforting, nutritious pots of soup. And to the winter of 2014/15 for being so very challenging (with all that relentless snow and cold), so that making soup was one of the only things that got me through.

To Hope Murphy for thinking up this Soup Swap Supper idea so many years ago. The friendships and sense of community that have come through soup have been a revelation. To the entire Soup Swap Supper crew, many thanks for all the delicious pots of soup. Thank you Hope and Brad, Amy and Jon, Galen and Tod, Patty and Fred, Becky and Ben, and John.

Thanks to my editor, Amy Treadwell, for discovering my article about the Soup Swap Suppers in *Yankee* magazine and thinking this would make a great book. Thanks to Lorena Jones and the whole team at Chronicle Books who shaped my words, edited my recipes, and generally fine-tuned this manuscript: copy editor Brenda Goldberg, managing editor Doug Ogan, designer Alice Chau, production manager Tera Killip, and publicist Amy Cleary. Thanks to Yvonne Duivenvoorden for the gorgeous photography.

Thanks to my agent Doe Coover for making this book happen and taking care of all the details. And also for patting me on the back when I ended up getting the manuscript in on time!

Thanks to Joe Yonan, Grace Young, John and Jane Angelopolos, Hope Murphy, Maya Rudolph, and Emma Rudolph for the great recipes. Many thanks to Karen Mazzari for the great day spent making posole. And special thanks to Stephanie Deihl for her delicious recipe and her invaluable help retesting the soup recipes.

Thanks to the women in my writers' group who cheer me on and help me form better, clearer sentences: Marie Harris, Susan Poulin, Mimi White, and Grace Mattern.

Thanks to Davia Nelson for letting us stay in her San Francisco apartment and to Elisa Newman for sharing her California kitchen, where I created several of these soups. Thanks to Karen Frillmann for all the love and support.

Thanks to my mother-in-law, Nancy Rudolph, who taught me so much about the pleasures of the kitchen.

Mostly, as always, thanks to my family. John, you are always there, always hungry, and always so full of love and encouragement. And to Maya and Emma, for your love, your great ideas, and the wonderful unique ways you both support your mother. A special shout-out to Emma Rudolph for all the time she took going over this manuscript so *very* carefully. It's so appreciated, Em.